THE CHAPEL PERILOUS

Dorothy Hewett

Currency Press,
Sydney

CURRENCY PLAYS

First published in 1972
by Currency Press Pty Ltd
PO Box 2287, Strawberry Hills, NSW, 2012, Australia
enquiries@currency.com.au
www.currency.com.au

Reprinted 1972 (4 times), 1973, 1977, 1981, 1985, 1988, 1992, 1996, 2007, 2009, 2016, 2023

NATIONAL LIBRARY OF AUSTRALIA CIP DATA

Hewett, Dorothy, 1923-2002.
  The chapel perilous : or, the perilous adventures of Sally Banner.
  Rev. ed.
  ISBN 9780868198149 (pbk.).
  1. Women - Drama. I. Title.
  A822.3
Typeset by Dean Nottle for Currency Press.
Cover artwork by Peter Long; cover design by Kate Florance, Currency Press
Front cover shows Dorothy Hewett.

Currency Press acknowledges the Traditional Owners of the Country on which we live and work. We pay our respects to all Aboriginal and Torres Strait Islander Elders, past and present.

Contents

THE CHAPEL PERILOUS

Prologue   1

Act One   23

Act Two   52

Glossary   87

The Chapel Perilous derives from Sir Thomas Malory's The Tale of King Arthur, 1485 (Winchester MS, Caxton, Book VI).

HOW SIR LAUNCELOT CAM INTO THE CHAPEL PERELUS AND GATE THERE OF A DED CORPS, A PYECE OF THE CLOTH AND A SWORDE

Than she sayde, 'Sir, folow ye evyn this hygheway, and hit woll brynge you to the Chapel Perelus, and here I shall abyde till God sende you agayne. And yf you spede nat I know no knyght lyvynge that may encheve that adventure.

Ryght so sir Launcelot departed, and when he com to the Chapel Perelus he alyght downe and tyed his horse unto a lytyll gate. And as sone as he was within the chyrche yerde he sawe on the frunte of the chapel many fayre ryche shyldis turned up so downe, and many of the shyldis sir Launcelot had sene knyghtes bere byforehande. With that he sawe by hym there stonde a thirty grete knyghtes, more by a yerde than any man that ever he had sene, and all they greened and gnasted at sir Launcelot. And whan he sawe their contenaunce he dredde hym sore, and so put his shylde before hym and toke his swerde in his honde redy unto batayle.

And they all were armed all in blak harneyse, redy with her shyldis and her swerdis redy drawyn. And as sir Launcelot wolde have gone thorow them they skaterd on every syde of hym and gaff hym the way, and therewith he wexed bolde and entyrde into the chapel. And there he sawe no lyght but a dymme lampe brennyng, and than was he ware of a corpus hylled with a clothe of sylke. Than sir Launcelot stouped doune and kutte a pese away of that cloth, and than hit fared undir hym as the grounde had quaked a lytyll; therewithall he feared.

And than he sawe a fayre swerde lye by the dede knyght, and that he gate in his honde and hyed hym oute of the chapel. Anone as ever he was in the chapel yerde all the knyghtes spake to hym with grymly voyces and seyde, 'Knyght, sir Launcelot, lay that swerde frome the or thou shalt dye!'

'Whether that I lyve other dye,' seyde sir Launcelot, 'with no wordys grete gete ye hit agayne. Therefore fyght for hit and ye lyst.'

Than ryght so he passed throwoute them.

The Chapel Perilous was first performed at the New Fortune Theatre, Perth, on 21 January 1971, with the following cast:

SALLY BANNER	Helen Neeme
MICHAEL	Colin Nugent
THOMAS / FATHER	Clifford Holden
SISTER ROSA / JUDITH / DAVID / SAUL	Victor Marsh
HEADMISTRESS / MOTHER	Margaret Ford

with Penny Allsop, Brian Blain, William Clark, Charlotte Connell, Trudy Edmonds, David Heeley, Emma Hogen-Esch, Penny Leech, Rick Mackay Scollay, Adele Marcella, Marianne Megan, Howard Nowak, Elizabeth Rafferty, Patrick Rafferty, Tricia Robbins, Rosemary Sands, Miles Smith, Grant Synnot, Teresa Ungvary.

Original music composed by Frank Arndt and Michael Leyden

Directed by Aarne Neeme
Setting designed by Brian Blain
Musical direction by Frank Arndt

ACKNOWLEDGEMENTS

We are indebted to the following publishers for kind permission to quote from works under copyright: Constable & Co. Ltd, 'Ringsend (after reading Tolstoy)', by Oliver St John Gogarty; Jonathon Cape Ltd, 'Come Live with Me and Be My Love', by Cecil Day Lewis; Cambridge University Press, 'To a Fat Lady Seen from a Train' by Frances Cornford. Other poems appearing in the text are by Dorothy Hewett with the exception of 'Overtime Rock' by Les Flood; 'Shadows On The Wall' by Michael Leyden; and certain popular and classical works familiar to the reader, including 'For the Fallen' by Laurence Binyon; 'Jerusalem' by William Blake; 'The Bait' by John Donne; 'Invictus' by W.E. Henley. We also acknowledge the kind permission of Eyre and Spottiswoode (Publishers) Ltd, to quote the extract from Patrick White, *The Burnt Ones*.

CHARACTERS

SALLY BANNER, from fifteen to sixty one years old, a poet. Most of her scenes are played as a young woman: handsome, long haired, rebellious, self absorbed.

THOMAS, from his twenties to forties. Sally's husband: idealistic, gullible.

MICHAEL, seventeen to forties. Her lover: rough, demanding, cruel.

DAVID, twenties to forties. Her lover: university student and biologist, an intellectual.

SAUL, in his thirties. Her lover: a leader of the Communist Party of Australia, an authority figure.

JUDITH, a schoolgirl and later a teaching nun: sardonic, cold, lesbian.

HEADMISTRESS, an English bluestocking with intellect and dignity.

CANON, ageing, weak, hypocritical.

SISTER ROSA, a senior member of an Anglican teaching order: an implacable authority figure.

MOTHER, from middle age to senility: neurotic and overbearing.

FATHER, middle aged and sad.

Other female characters: UNIVERSITY STUDENTS, NURSES, MISS FUNT, SCHOOLGIRLS, MICKY SNATCHIT, POLICEWOMAN, FEMALE SPRUIKER

Other male characters: UNIVERSITY STUDENTS, INTERNES, POLICEMEN, RADIO ANNOUNCERS, VARIOUS VOICES, PALLBEARERS, PSYCHOLOGIST, MAGISTRATE, OLD TRAMP, SPRUIKERS

CHORUS of singers and dancers, male and female: schoolgirls, students, protesters. They are essentially chorus crowd figures

The play has been performed successfully with two women and four men playing all the bit parts and the chorus. A separate chorus is, of course, preferable.

SETTING

A permanent set. Upstage against the cyclorama is the outline of a school chapel with a stained-glass window discovered later to contain a figure of Sally Banner. Three shallow steps lead to the chapel and the tower is accessible. In front of the chapel are three rostrums and an altar on a platform. Large masks of the Headmistress, the Canon and Sister Rosa remain constant throughout the play, standing on the three rostrums and large enough to hide an actor behind each. Three loudspeakers are placed prominently.

The three masked figures play the roles of judges of the action against the landscape of the profane chapel. Sometimes they play themselves, sometimes they step from behind the masks into the body of the play and become other characters.

PROLOGUE

The stage is in darkness.

A clap of thunder rolls away.

Ushers in school uniforms and the rest of the cast take up their positions.

SALLY: I rode forward through the blackened land. I found the forests burning and the fields wasted, waiting for rain. Upon a slope I saw a glimpse of light. Then I came to the Chapel Perilous.

> *Loud knocking.*

> *The chant begins.*

CHORUS: [*in the auditorium*] God give thee comfort, poor soul. Whither goest thou this night?

SALLY: I seek the Chapel Perilous and by my courage and great heart I will win through.

> *Loud knocking.*

CHORUS: Sorrow and death, rebellion and treachery stalk the land. Who are ye who are neither pure in heart nor humble?

SALLY: I have seen such things that are beyond the power of the tongue to describe or the heart to recall, and had I not sinned I would have seen much more.

CHORUS: Your worldly renown can avail thee nothing in matter of the spirit. Repent yet for ye do not belong to the blessed, and we foretell your death.

> *Blackout.* SALLY *exits.*

> *The chant fades away and lights come up.*

> *The outline of the chapel is revealed with its large stained-glass window representing the figure of* SALLY BANNER. *The altar is dressed with cloth and candles.*

HEADMISTRESS: [*coming from behind her mask*] Parents, teachers, girls: on this speech day we pause to honour one who was once of your number, who walked these same lawns, carrying her books; who seemed, on the face of it, to be much as you are now; young, unsure, adolescent, facing the problems of life. Yet she *was* different from all of you and her teachers felt the difference even then. It is rarely given to meet a student who has the recognisable instant quality... genius... major poet.

AMPLIFIER: [HEADMISTRESS*'s voice*] Minor poet! Major poet in a provincial town.

HEADMISTRESS: These are big words yet we began to apply them to her while she was still in her teens.

AMPLIFIER: [HEADMISTRESS*'s voice*] Big frog in a small puddle.

HEADMISTRESS: We were all privileged to know her and as I look about this great hall inscribed with the names of famous women in history I rejoice that the name of my old pupil stands amongst them.

   A spot lights SALLY.

SALLY: Queen Elizabeth, Madame Curie, Florence Nightingale, Jane Austen, Emily Brontë, Joan of Arc, Boadicea, Grace Darling, Queen Victoria, Elizabeth Fry, Helen Keller, Daisy Bates... [*Whispering*] Sally Banner... Sally Banner...

HEADMISTRESS: I believe I always knew it would be so.

SCHOOLGIRLS: [*singing*] Poor Sally.
   She never made it.
   No matter how hard she tried.
   She tried hard not to know it,
   But she *was* a minor poet,
   Until the day she died.

HEADMISTRESS: I remember her fragile, passionate poems in the school magazine, the range and depth of reading that gave her a gold medal for English in her final examinations. I remember her delicate, sardonic school essays for which she always received...

AMPLIFIER: [HEADMISTRESS'*s voice, angrily*] I feel incapable of evaluating this.

HEADMISTRESS: [*firmly*] Always received A-minus.

AMPLIFIER: [HEADMISTRESS*'s voice*] You seem to be in danger of regarding literature as a drug addict regards his drug, a perpetual stimulant to unreality.

HEADMISTRESS: Beware of rhetoric.

AMPLIFIER: [HEADMISTRESS*'s voice*] *Put your name in your book!*

HEADMISTRESS: She was an impossible child to teach. One never really reached her. She would sit for hours in class never listening to a word I said.

AMPLIFIER: [HEADMISTRESS's *voice*] I must warn you. She is in moral danger, and a danger to others.

HEADMISTRESS: Yet one always knew even when she was at her most outrageous that here was a superlative gift and talent.

AMPLIFIER: [HEADMISTRESS's *voice*] She is morbid, introspective, violent, immature, dangerous, malicious, macabre… and *lesbian*.

HEADMISTRESS: I feel incapable of evaluating this. [*With an amplifier, as through an echo chamber*] I feel incapable… incapable… incapable… of evaluating this… *this… this… this…*

The CANON *comes from behind his mask.*

CANON: Parents, teachers, young ladies, dear brethren, children of Christ; on this speech day, we pause to honour Sally Banner, born Widgiemooltha, 1923. As canon of this college of young and foolish virgins, I bear a great responsibility, and I rejoice today that we are gathered together here to offer up our humble thanks to Miss Banner, who has so liberally endowed our little chapel with a stained-glass window in her image and likeness… as well as providing some little patrimony for me. For since the days when she walked amongst you, an upright and Christian young woman, Miss Banner has travelled one of the great symbolic journeys of the human spirit. And she has come home at last to her beginnings, to the Mother Church that bore her, to the Chapel Perilous where at last we all must come. Dear friends, let us pray… I believe in the Holy Ghost, the Holy Catholic Church, the Communion of Saints, the forgiveness…

Amplifiers and the CHORUS OF GIRLS *join in the creed, which continues under the amplifier.*

AMPLIFIER: [CANON's *voice*] I don't remember any Sally Banner. Who was this Sally Banner? Was she thin, fat, blonde, brunette or redhead, bad, good or indifferent?

The CHORUS *recital stops.*

CANON: I baptised her, confirmed her, married her, from this very chapel. Some of the old girls present would have caught a belladonna lily from her bridal bouquet.

AMPLIFIER: [CANON's *voice*] God knows! I'm an old man, and all that I remember is that I married my dead wife's sister. She was a young thing then, lived with us all our married life. My wife was scarcely cold.

CANON: *The forgiveness of sins, the resurrection of the body and the life everlasting!*

> *The* CHORUS *responds.*

AMPLIFIER: [CANON's *voice*] It was forbidden in the Anglican Church. But I received a dispensation. She had such breasts on her.

CANON: I believe in God, the Father Almighty, the maker of heaven and earth, and in Jesus Christ his only son our Lord, conceived by the Virgin Mary, suffered under Pontius Pilate, was crucified…

> *The* CHORUS *continues under the amplifier.*

CHORUS: Dead and buried. He descended into hell. The third day he arose again from the dead, he ascended into Heaven and sits at the right hand of God, the Father Almighty, from thence he shall come to judge the living and the dead.

AMPLIFIER: [CANON's *voice*] They crucified me. There was a scandal and I nearly lost my living. Oh! I remember how they sat and giggled. Nasty little females, sitting in the pews with their wet thighs pressed together. And she amongst them… Sally Banner.

CANON: Crucified, dead and buried.

CHORUS: Crucified, dead and buried.

AMPLIFIER: [CANON's *voice*] And it was all for nothing. She turned out dry as the other one.

CANON: Life everlasting… life everlasting…

CHORUS: Life everlasting… life everlasting…

AMPLIFIER: [CANON's *voice*] Wet thighs pressed together.

CANON: Crucified, dead and buried…

CHORUS: Crucified, dead and buried.

AMPLIFIER: [CANON's *voice*] Dry as the other one…

CANON: Amen.

> SISTER ROSA *comes from behind her mask.*

SISTER ROSA: Parents, teachers, girls: on this speech day I welcome back our old pupil, Sally Banner, who was once one of your number, who walked in the school crocodile to the school chapel, who curtseyed before the altar, and bowed to the name of Jesus. Her name appears, suitably inscribed in bold type, in the school prospectus. An old woman remembers only those pupils who have made some mark in the world: I remember Sally Banner. I remember her well.

AMPLIFIER: [SISTER ROSA's *voice*] I remember her bold eyes staring me down at the foot of the altar. She would not bow. She would not bow...

SISTER ROSA: She was not baptised, nor confirmed. Therefore she could never become a school prefect.

AMPLIFIER: [SISTER ROSA's *voice*] She drew lewd women on the back of her divinity notebook, and she would not bow. *She would not bow.*

SISTER ROSA: She had a slight tendency to wildness, never wearing her hat to the school tuck shop, and occasionally found out of bounds. She had no school spirit.

AMPLIFIER: [SISTER ROSA's *voice*] Adulteress, divorced, she lived in sin. She did not bow, she did not bow.

SALLY: [*young, fresh, joyous*] I will live in Ringsend
With a red-headed whore,
And the fan-light gone in
Where it lights the hall door.

SISTER ROSA: Sally, Sally Banner, where did you find that awful verse?

SALLY: Why, Sister Rosa, in the *Oxford Book of Modern Verse* I got for the English prize.

AMPLIFIER: [SISTER ROSA's *voice*] *And she did not bow... She did not bow...*

> *A bell rings.* SCHOOLGIRLS *come from all parts of the school and take up positions on right and left of stage.*

GIRLS: [*singing*] Bring me my bow of burning gold:
Bring me my arrows of desire:
Bring me my spear! Oh! clouds unfold:
Bring me my chariot of fire!
I will not cease from mental fight,
Nor shall my sword sleep in my hand:
'Til we have built Jerusalem,
In England's green and pleasant land.

The hymn tails off as SALLY BANNER *enters down the centre aisle, singing. She goes to the altar and stands before it.* SISTER ROSA *stands beside the altar, arms folded.* SALLY *confronts her.*

SISTER ROSA: Bow.

>   SALLY *remains rigid with her back to the audience.*

Go back, that girl. Make your entrance again. 'Bring me your bow…', girls, please.

>   SALLY *retreats up the aisle. The* GIRLS *repeat the hymn.* SALLY *comes again to stand rigid at the altar.*

Bow.

>   SALLY *remains rigid.*

Again, Sally Banner. Girls, *please*: 'I will not cease from mental fight…'

>   SALLY *retreats, then returns.*

Bow.

SALLY: I will live in Ringsend with a red-headed whore.

>   *Pause.* SISTER ROSA *exits behind her mask. The stage darkens, with a spotlight on* SALLY *who sits in front of the altar, cross-legged. The* SCHOOLGIRLS *slowly dance around her, singing softly.*

GIRLS: Come live with me and be my love,
          And we will some new pleasures prove
          Of golden sands and crystal brooks,
          With silken lines and silver hooks.
          There will the river whispering run,
          Warmed by thy eyes more than the sun.
          And there the enamoured fish will stay.
          Begging themselves they may betray.

>   *They sit in a circle to watch the next scene. Their voices die away. The stage darkens further.*

>   *The heads of the* CANON *and the* HEADMISTRESS *are silhouetted by a red glow.* JUDITH, *hair cropped, in school uniform, enters from behind* SISTER ROSA*'s mask. She stands behind the altar.*

SALLY: [*rising*] Judith, is that you, Judith?

JUDITH: Bow.

> *She moves forward and presses* SALLY *'s head down before altar.* SALLY *presses her face into* JUDITH *'s knees.*

SALLY: I'll bow to you. From the first moment I saw you, sitting at the back of the schoolroom in winter with the fire on your face, I knew I loved you.

JUDITH: Be careful. Somebody will hear you.

SALLY: I'd like to take you in my arms and shake some feeling into you, you cold, cold bitch. I want to feel everything. To tell everything, to walk naked. That's my protection.

JUDITH: That's a cold comfort, Sally.

SALLY: Nobody can touch you then.

JUDITH: I can't claim something I don't even feel.

SALLY: Why do you always tell such huge lies? Don't go. Where are you going? Don't you see? I want it like this… perilous and terrible. Judith, it's only a friendship… a strange friendship.

JUDITH: Haven't you seen them nudging when girls have crushes on mistresses?

SALLY: Oh, for Christ's sake, let them nudge, then. You're beautiful: 'Beautiful as the flying legend of some leopard'.

JUDITH: What are you saying now?

SALLY: I'm saying, coward, that I love you. I'm saying, coward, that I ache for you to be a man. I'm saying, coward, that that queer, affected voice of yours drives me mad, so that I could punch your mouth and kiss you 'til the blood comes. I'm saying, coward, that I hate your smug invention of a mind that finds pleasure in illicit loving as long as it's not mentioned outright.

JUDITH: Don't dare.

SALLY: The presents I buy you, the press of the hand, the deepness in the eyes, the pain in the voice, even the thigh against yours, that's all right, isn't it, as long as it's not too explicit? Haven't you ever trembled with my hand against your knee?

JUDITH: Yes.

SALLY: Or is it only the poetry I write you? Does that feed you?

JUDITH: It feeds me.

SALLY: You want me to be like the others… afraid and secretive?

JUDITH: No.

They move together. SALLY *touches her face.*

If only I could reach past your body to you.

SALLY: Don't be afraid, Jude. You're my heart, my breath, my body's warmth. [*Kissing her*] I see you always in your blue shirt with your shaggy head outlined against the sky. Do you remember that day we went on the geology expedition, and walked through that old churchyard with the graves of twin children under the two poplar trees?

    They sit hunched together. SALLY *has her head in* JUDITH's *lap.*

Oh, Jude, why were you a woman?

JUDITH: If we went across the paddocks to the river bank…

SALLY: We could lie there all night in each other's arms. Oh, Jude, what bliss. Nobody would ever miss us.

HEADMISTRESS: [*from the dais*] Judith, Judith, may I speak to you a moment, dear?

JUDITH: Get up, Sally, get up, it's Mrs Lou.

SALLY: I'll wait for you in front of the chapel after lights-out.

JUDITH: I didn't mean it. I was only teasing.

SALLY: Oh no, you weren't. I'll wait for you there… all night if necessary. And this time, Jude, if you don't come I think I'll kill you.

    SALLY *moves upstage until she is only a shadow in front of the chapel.*

HEADMISTRESS: Is that you, Judith? I thought I heard voices.

JUDITH: It's only me, Mrs Lou.

    Long awkward pause.

HEADMISTRESS: Judith, I don't know how to open up this conversation. I'm an ageing woman and I've seen a good deal of the world.

JUDITH: Yes, Mrs Lou.

HEADMISTRESS: People are very complex, particularly gifted people. [*Pause.*] There is a girl here in this school, a very gifted girl but a dangerous one, dangerous to herself but particularly to other girls. I have to warn you. It is my duty. Are you listening?

JUDITH: I don't really understand what you mean.

HEADMISTRESS: I think you do. I found this… this… diary in Sally's desk this morning.

JUDITH: You searched her desk? You spied on her?

HEADMISTRESS: I found it necessary. I would like to read it to you.

JUDITH: Don't read it to me.

HEADMISTRESS: But you're going to hear it because it concerns you, it concerns the rest of your lives. Listen… listen, Judith.

SALLY: I'm in love with a girl, a flat-chested, boyish-looking girl and because it can have nothing but a tragic end I'm prepared to exhaust the last scalding drop out of it. Whatever tricks I have to use, whatever pretences I have to make, whatever frigidity I have to assume, I'll do it. Nobody must know, not the sharp, pricking eyes of the girls, not the savage, hooded eyes of Sister Rosa, or even the eyes of Judith herself. Particularly it must be hidden from Judith herself, who could never face such knowledge. She must be protected from all its implications.

> *Pause.*

HEADMISTRESS: I could have this girl expelled from the school.

JUDITH: You're against Sally.

HEADMISTRESS: I find Sally… unwholesome, both precocious and evil. I really can't bear that much individuality. It frightens me and it should frighten you.

JUDITH: It does frighten me.

HEADMISTRESS: She is not a friend… for normal people.

JUDITH: She is my friend.

HEADMISTRESS: When the time comes Sally will leave you without the courtesy of a backward glance.

JUDITH: I can't lose Sally.

HEADMISTRESS: You force my hand, Judith.

JUDITH: I need Sally.

HEADMISTRESS: What would your mother think, snapping the heads off her dead roses beside the river and reading *Sonnets from the Portuguese*?

> JUDITH *is laughing and laughing.*

What would your father think with his long, kind sheep's head in a grey business suit, member of the legislature, inheritor of the ancestral acres? What would your sister think, riding with hauteur to hounds in a black bowler hat, and a silver cup on the mantelshelf to show for it every year? You will not go to the chapel. You will not speak to Sally again tonight.

JUDITH: Leave her there waiting all night?

HEADMISTRESS: All night... if necessary.

JUDITH: Yes.

HEADMISTRESS: Your relationship is over; no weekend visits, no long strolls by the river bank; I never want to see your heads together again on the school lawn by the swimming pool.

JUDITH: Reading poetry.

HEADMISTRESS: Reading poetry. I'm waiting for your word.

JUDITH: Yes.

HEADMISTRESS: This has not been pleasant for me, Judith.

> *The* HEADMISTRESS *moves aside.* JUDITH *sinks down before altar.*

SALLY: [*mocking in front of the chapel*]
> O why do you walk through the fields in gloves,
> Missing so much and so much?
> O fat white woman whom nobody loves,
> Why do you walk through the fields in gloves,
> When the grass is soft as the breast of doves
> And shivering-sweet to the touch?

> *Schoolgirl laughter.*

GIRLS: O why do you walk through the fields in gloves,
> Missing so much and so much?

> *Peals of laughter.*

SALLY: Jude, I'm waiting, Jude.

JUDITH: I'm not coming, Sally... not coming ever again.

SALLY: Why do you torment me?

JUDITH: This is the end of it.

SALLY: Why?

JUDITH: Because you're precocious and... evil and I really can't bear this much individuality.

SALLY: It frightens you?

JUDITH: It sickens me. I find you... unwholesome.

SALLY: You love me.

JUDITH: Absurd, melodramatic and fairly comic.

JUDITH *moves back behind the rostrum mask of* SISTER ROSA.

SALLY: O small dark head against the sky
And your throat with the blue shirt and the boy's body,
Why were you a woman?

SALLY *begins to climb the chapel tower. As she climbs the* GIRLS *sing.*

GIRLS: Dear hypocrite, why is my love for you
So bright and bold, so burning bright?
I hate you and your bow to smart convention.
I hate your smug invention of a mind.
Dear hypocrite, I ask myself one question.
Why is my love for you so blind?
Why is my love for you so blind?

SALLY *can be seen outlined in the chapel tower. Chapel bells ring.*

FIRST GIRL: Sally Banner is climbing the chapel tower.

SECOND GIRL: Why is she up so high?

FIRST GIRL: She's out on the parapet now.

SECOND GIRL: Sally Banner's going to fall from the top of the chapel tower.

CANON: [*running from his mask*] Ring out, wild bells. What is all the commotion in the school chapel tonight, my dears? All the foolish virgins! What a responsibility it is. Sally Banner [*peering up*], come down out of the chapel tower. It's sacrilege and you'll catch your death.

SISTER ROSA: [*running from her mask*] Sally Banner, Chamberlain's back from Munich. Come down out of the chapel tower. It's peace in our time and raspberry cordial for afternoon tea.

HEADMISTRESS: [*waddling from her mask*] Sally Banner, come down out of the chapel tower. It's the last day of peace and that foolish man with the umbrella has betrayed us all.

The figures freeze, gazing up at SALLY.

AMPLIFIER: [SALLY'*s voice*] You know I nearly died. I nearly died out of the top window of the cloisters at school. Nobody will ever believe me but it was so close. But I didn't go. I wasn't quite as weak and hopeless as that. Just one off.

The bells ring wildly. SALLY *drops her hat from the tower.* GIRLS *run about screaming. Big Ben chimes. The* HEADMISTRESS *takes off her academic gown and puts on an apron, becoming* MOTHER. CANON *takes off his robe, becoming* FATHER. SISTER ROSA *goes back to the rostrum.* MOTHER *carries knitting and a chair to the front of the stage.* FATHER *carries a chair and newspaper to the front of the stage.* SALLY *runs down from the chapel tower and sits cross-legged between them, writing in an exercise book.*

AMPLIFIER: [BRITISH PRIME MINISTER CHAMBERLAIN's *voice*] I am speaking to you from the Cabinet room of Ten Downing Street. This morning the British Ambassador to Berlin handed the German Government a final note stating that unless we heard from them by eleven o'clock that they were prepared, at once, to withdraw their troops from Poland, a state of war would exist between us; I have to tell you that no such undertaking has been received.

FATHER: Sally, put down your book and listen. This is history.

MOTHER: Why don't you do what your father asks?

FATHER: Can you hear me, Sally?

MOTHER: Always making trouble.

FATHER: I'll make you listen.

He hurls the exercise book onto the floor.

SALLY: I don't want to listen.

MOTHER: He'll make you listen.

SALLY: It's nothing to do with me.

FATHER: Have a bit of decency.

MOTHER: Born at dawn by forceps in Widgiemooltha, and there wasn't a flying doctor.

FATHER: Tommy rot.

AMPLIFIER: Consequently this country is at war with Germany.

FATHER: Listen !

SALLY: I read *All Quiet on the Western Front.*

MOTHER: He won the Croix de Guerre.

AMPLIFIER: You can imagine what a bitter blow it is to me that all my long struggle to win peace has failed.

MOTHER: Why, the King of the Belgians kissed him on both his cheeks.

AMPLIFIER: We have a clear conscience. We have done all any country could do to establish peace.

MOTHER: He won the Distinguished Conduct Medal. I polish it every year with Brasso on Anzac Day.

SALLY: I'm a pacifist.

MOTHER: You can knit all the socks you want to, now.

FATHER: Go to bed; if you won't listen, you can go to bed.

AMPLIFIER: Now God bless you all. May He defend the right. It is the evil thing that we shall be fighting against. Brute force, bad faith, injustice, oppression and persecution…

MOTHER: She doesn't understand. She's only a child.

FATHER: Too big for her boots.

AMPLIFIER: And against these I am sure that right will prevail.

FATHER: The war to end war.

> MOTHER *picks up the exercise book and reads from it.*

MOTHER: 'He laughed and pulled my skirt above my hips,
And drank again of my soft yielding lips.'
Father, Father, for God's sake read this. It's Sally. She's a wild girl. She's a dirty little whore.

SALLY: I believe in the blood and the flesh as being wiser than the intellect.

FATHER: I believe in a good smacked bottom.

MOTHER: She was frightened when she first saw the blood. I hadn't told her. It always makes me feel better, I said, when I think the Queen is a woman and has to put up with it too.

AMPLIFIER: Now God bless us all. I'm sure that right will prevail.

MOTHER: I told her about sex. I've always thought it was a dirty business, I said. They found a man and woman stuck together on the Esplanade. Just like two dogs. He was too big for her and her insides came down. They had to cut it off. Terrible things happen.

FATHER: Listen! Once outside that little village in France we had to dig through five layers of bodies to make a trench. Five layers of frozen bodies. Five layers of winters, arms kept dropping off, legs kept snapping off. The stench was bad.

> *He sings.*

Tiddley-iddley itey,
Carry me back to Blighty,
Blighty is the place for me.

SALLY: I am sixteen years old. I am a Gemini. I am pretty but I am
    something more than that. All I want is to be a great actress and
    a great writer. Sometimes I sing, too, and I spend a lot of time
    drawing women with slanted eyes and long tousled hair. People
    do not approve of me but I fascinate them. My teacher calls me a
    poseur and the girls think I am trying to be different. Some of them
    think I am a genius and so do I.
FATHER: If you won't listen, go to bed.

> SALLY *moves far right, with her back to the audience.*
>
> *A few bars of 'God Save the King'.*
>
> FATHER *and* MOTHER *stand stiffly to attention, then sit.*

FIRST GIRL: Sister, Sally Banner takes off her black stockings and meets
    a man with a violin at the school gates every night.
SECOND GIRL: [*giggling*] What does he do with his violin?
FIRST GIRL: He plays 'Souvenirs' off-key when the sun goes down.
SECOND GIRL: And he's actually *twenty-two*.
FIRST GIRL: He's a Catholic so he only feels her breasts.
AMPLIFIER: [*a man's voice, breathing hard*] I might take your chastity
    but I'll never take your virginity.

> *A* SCHOOLGIRL *giggles.*

You're a dangerous sort of woman, darling.
SECOND GIRL: She buys a sixpenny lipstick at the corner chemist. It
    flakes off like black blood on her lips.

> FATHER *sits in a spot reading his paper.* MOTHER *sits beside him
> knitting a shapeless garment like a shroud.*
>
> *Jazz syncopation; a male voice on the amplifier, singing; bad
> fiddle accompaniment off key; the* GIRLS *dance.*

AMPLIFIER: [*a man's voice*]
> You're a dangerous sort of woman, darling,
> In the back seat of a car.
> You're a dangerous sort of woman, darling,
> No matter where you are.
> We buttoned the side curtains snugly in my
> Fast little cheap sports car,
> And there's no doubt you're gaol-bait, darling,
> Though we didn't go very far.

MOTHER: [*knitting savagely*] She meets him after school every night.

FATHER: [*rustling paper*] Nag, nag, nag.

MOTHER: He's a Catholic. They can do anything, as long as they confess it.

FATHER: What's she see in him?

MOTHER: It's the violin. She likes the violin.

FATHER: He can't even bloody well tune it.

MOTHER: She's capable of anything.

FATHER: Fix his little caper.

MOTHER: She'd have to turn.

MAGISTRATE: [*entering from behind the altar*] Sally Banner?

AMPLIFIER: Sally Banner.

SCHOOLGIRLS: [*whispering together*] Sally Banner.

MAGISTRATE: Is Sally Banner in the court?

AMPLIFIER: Call poor bloody Sally.

MAGISTRATE: Silence in the court. Call Sally Banner.

ALL: Sally Banner! [*Whispering*] Sally Banner, Sally Banner, Sally Banner.

> FATHER *pushes* SALLY *towards the* MAGISTRATE *as she walks somnambulistically to the rostrum.* MOTHER *trots after. They stand on either side of* SALLY, *supporting or restraining her.*

MAGISTRATE: Sally Banner charged under the Act with being an uncontrollable child. Anything to say?

GIRLS & SALLY: [*together*] Nothing, Your Honour.

MAGISTRATE: [*pulling out a long charge sheet, unrolling it as he reads*] Sally Banner went with a Catholic, disobeyed her parents on the back seat of his car, buttoned the side curtains, lost her chastity, cracked the mica, but kept her virginity. Luck of the draw. How do you plead?

GIRLS & SALLY [*together*] Guilty, Your Honour.

MAGISTRATE: Sally Banner, placed on probation in the care of your parents to walk circumspectly all the days of your life. Never to meet at the school gates at evening a young man in a sports car who plays 'Souvenirs'.

AMPLIFIER: [*a man's voice to an off-key violin solo*]
I find a broken heart,
Among my souvenirs.

A violin string snaps.

FATHER: Poor little girl. My poor silly little girl.

SALLY: [*coming downstage*] Well, I guess there's a phantom groper in everybody's past.

> SALLY *is in a pale spot on the darkened stage.*

But Michael wasn't a phantom. He was a real boy. He rode past me on a bike in the second year of the War.

> *'Begin the Beguine' can be heard faintly.*

I must have been in school uniform. I know I felt dark and my hair must have been long and fair and my face pale. He came riding round the corner, suddenly, with his head bent over the handlebars. Everybody rode bikes then. I remember his face, very pale, and it floated over his body. I can't remember anything except his head, the fair, straight hair and the extraordinarily sullen mouth and eyes. It was by that wattle tree on the edge of the street. I think it had been raining, because the road seemed to be very blue and wet.

> *She puts on a white raincoat.* MICHAEL *enters from left in shorts, shirt and raincoat, a rough, strong-looking boy with a sullen face. He rides a bicycle. He stops opposite* SALLY, *puts her in front of him and rides to the far left of the stage. The scene is covered by the following dialogue.*

FIRST GIRL: Sister, Sally Banner's got another one.

SECOND GIRL: She's meeting a rough boy on a bicycle deep in the grass by the school gates every night.

FIRST GIRL: He takes off her clothes and he kisses her… all over.

SECOND GIRL: She's lost her chastity.

FIRST GIRL: He's taken her virginity.

> *Lights up on* SALLY *and* MICHAEL.

SALLY: I brought you *Wuthering Heights*.

MICHAEL: What is it?

SALLY: It's a book, a marvellous book. Look. I've even written in it: 'To my Heathcliff from your Cathy'.

> MICHAEL *gazes puzzled at the flyleaf.* SALLY *tries to snatch the book back.*

It's absurd, isn't it? You don't even understand it, do you?

MICHAEL: It doesn't matter. I'll always keep it.

He stows it in his bike carrier.

SALLY: Warm rain!

MICHAEL: Come in under the tree. The leaves are soft.

SALLY: It's a scratchy bed.

They laugh together and kiss.

We have this, haven't we, whatever happens, I have this. Look, there's a dead leaf blowing over your hand. I can hear the river running. Do you think we'll always remember this night? Will you?

MICHAEL: [*kissing her*] You talk too much. Talk's cheap.

SALLY: Years from now when you see that star move across the sky will you remember me, or will you say: 'Where was I when I saw that star? Who was that girl in my arms?'

MICHAEL: I'll remember what girl you were.

SALLY: What girl am I?

MICHAEL: My girl. Say it. Your girl.

SALLY: Your girl … always.

MICHAEL: You shivered.

SALLY: Somebody walked over my grave. Promise you won't leave me?

MICHAEL: [*stopping her*] We're alive now. You're in my arms. That's enough. Nobody can promise past that.

SALLY: No… nobody can promise more than that.

MICHAEL: So. Shut your mouth and take off your clothes.

She holds up her arms childishly and he takes her raincoat off.

The light shifts to MOTHER *and* FATHER *sitting stiffly.*

MOTHER: She's got another one now. She's at it again.

FATHER: She promised me she wouldn't think about boys 'til she was grown up. [*Pause.*] Perhaps she's grown up.

MOTHER: She's meeting him in the long grass on the river bank.

FATHER: She'll have to meet him here, where we can keep an eye on her.

FATHER *and* MOTHER *stand sentinel behind chairs.* FATHER *calls.*

Sally…

MOTHER: … come home.

FATHER: We want to keep our eyes on you.

> SALLY *and* MICHAEL *walk expressionlessly hand-in-hand to chairs.* SALLY *sits with* FATHER *standing behind her.* MICHAEL *sits with* MOTHER *standing behind him. They look straight ahead.*

SALLY: Don't leave me, Michael.

MICHAEL: I can't talk to you.

SALLY: They're destroying us.

MICHAEL: I can't stay here like this, Sally.

SALLY: Don't leave me alone.

MICHAEL: I feel trapped.

> FATHER *goes down to the front of the stage and winds the alarm clock.* MICHAEL *rises stiffly.*

I'm going now, Sally.

SALLY: [*in a low voice*] Wait for me under the wattle tree by the river and I'll come. I promise I'll come. If it takes years I'll come.

> MICHAEL *walks swiftly across the stage and takes his bike.* FATHER *grabs lumps of wood, stalks* MICHAEL *and tries to batter his skull.* MICHAEL *turns, the bike crashes. They grapple together.* FATHER *beats* MICHAEL's *skull and he falls.* MOTHER *and* FATHER *return to the rostrums.*

> FATHER *becomes the* CANON *again,* MOTHER *becomes the* HEADMISTRESS. SALLY *gets up slowly and painfully and moves to* MICHAEL.

Michael?

MICHAEL: Yes.

SALLY: It's not my fault.

MICHAEL: The bastard half killed me.

SALLY: They won't let me love you.

MICHAEL: I don't want you to love me.

SALLY: You don't want me anymore?

MICHAEL: Of course I want you. Will you do it with me again?

SALLY: Why?

MICHAEL: It's hard to find a girl who'll do it. I'm randy and I'm going to the War.

SALLY: Without promises?

MICHAEL: No promises.

SALLY: Without love.

MICHAEL: Without love.

> SALLY *begins taking off her clothes.*

SALLY: [*singing*] Without love I lay with you,
    Without love we coupled,
    Where the grass was wet with dew
    And my body troubled.
    I dropped my clothes,
    My heart I kept, secret as a bird,
    And when you lay down there with me,
    My heart you never heard.
    Unfaithfully I lay with you
    Where the grass was green,
    You never knew I lay beneath
    The lover you had been.
    Without love I lay with you.
    All my body troubled.
    Where the grass was wet with dew,
    Without love we coupled.

MICHAEL: [*head in hands*] I wanted you to refuse me, to say no!

SALLY: You wanted to destroy us.

MICHAEL: Why?

SALLY: Because you're so perverse and tormented, because you had to test us first to see if we existed.

MICHAEL: Why did you let me?

SALLY: I wanted to see if I could still love you lying on me like a dog.

MICHAEL: And could you?

SALLY: Yes.

MICHAEL: I can't love you after I've lain on you like a dog.

SALLY: No.

MICHAEL: I don't want you. I don't want you.

SALLY: Not now.

MICHAEL: So what does that make me?

SALLY: It means you failed the test, that's all.

MICHAEL: Why didn't you refuse? Why weren't you revolted, normal about it?

SALLY: I had to know. I couldn't go on pretending any longer.

MICHAEL: What did you want?

SALLY: A kind of… unique communion.

MICHAEL: And what have you got left?

SALLY: A unique desolation.

> MICHAEL *exits.* JUDITH *comes from behind her mask and stands, watching* SALLY.

JUDITH: What an awful little whore you are, Sally.

SALLY: He won't come back?

JUDITH: No, he won't.

SALLY: Why have *you* come?

JUDITH: I've often watched you together.

SALLY: Envious?

> JUDITH *slaps her face.* SALLY *begins to cry.*

He's left me. He won't come back.

JUDITH: [*with irony*] Dear hypocrite, why is my love for you so bright and bold, so burning bright?

> *She throws* SALLY *her blouse.*

Put your clothes on. [*Pause.*] You'll survive, Sally. You'll always survive… walking naked, crying to yourself. Look what she's doing now. Oh, look, look what she's doing now.

SALLY: [*putting on her blouse*] Jude, have you forgotten me?

JUDITH: Nobody forgets you, Sally.

> JUDITH *turns away.*

SALLY: Jude, stay with me.

JUDITH: No, I'm going too. You don't need me, Sally. You don't really need anyone… only you don't know it yet.

SALLY: I need myself, myself intact. Walking naked, that's a cold comfort, Jude.

JUDITH: Your choice, Sally.

> JUDITH *goes back to the rostrum and resumes the identity of* SISTER ROSA.

SALLY: [*reciting*] The dark fires shall burn in many rooms.
> Will you sometimes miss me with my tangled hair?
> Still girls in dark uniforms

Crouching in winter with their cold hands trembling,
Still voices echoing as our voices echoed
And the faded, frumped-up form of a mistress teaching French.
Does she remember us or do we pass
Only like dreams of dark figures,
Some with different hair and deep voices,
Or merely countless hats hanging on pegs,
Countless columns of moving, massed black legs.
Our minds are sprawled on unforbidden lawns,
Our voices lie like queer leaves in the clipped grass,
As we have believed, so we shall pass.

Lights come up. The AUTHORITY FIGURES *are in place.*

HEADMISTRESS: Sally Banner, it's speech day. Come up and get your
gold medal for English Literature.

> SALLY *moves to the* AUTHORITY FIGURES, *shaking hands. The*
> HEADMISTRESS *presents her gold medal.*

GIRLS: [*singing*] Bring me my bow of burning gold:
Bring me my arrows of desire…

AMPLIFIER: [SISTER ROSA*'s voice*] Sally Banner has not been baptised.
Therefore she will go straight to hell.

GIRLS: Bring me my spear! Oh! clouds unfold:
Bring me my chariot of fire!

AMPLIFIER: [CANON*'s voice*] Nasty little female with her wet thighs
pressed together.

GIRLS: I will not cease from Mental Fight,
Nor shall my Sword sleep in my hand…

AMPLIFIER: [HEADMISTRESS*'s voice*] Sally is a rebel in word and deed.
The latter usually tones with time.

GIRLS: 'Til we have built Jerusalem.

> *The* GIRLS*' voices on the amplifier modulate into a chant.*

With time, with time, with time… with time…

> *The* GIRLS *begin to march out.* SALLY *follows them, chanting.*

With time, with time, with time, with time…

> *The* AUTHORITY FIGURES *are left alone on stage. The stage*
> *darkens to a red glow, as the chapel bell tolls. The droning beat*

of the amplifier rises and dies away.
Time… time… time… time… time… time…

♦ ♦ ♦ ♦ ♦ ♦ ♦ ♦

ACT ONE

*We move straight into the music for Act One: pop tunes of the 1940s—
'Dark Town Strutters'Ball', 'In the Mood', 'Chattanooga Choo Choo',
'Tuxedo Junction'. The three authority masks are in place. The altar
has become a prop for holding costumes and other items.*

Enter dancing GIRLS *and* BOYS *dressed in the fashions of the 1940s.
Amongst them is* SALLY BANNER, *in red dress and flying beads. During
most of this scene the dancing figures remain constant, jitterbugging in
a frieze. The band plays 'Sympathy'.*

The voices of the AUTHORITY FIGURES *come through the amplifier.*

AMPLIFIER: [HEADMISTRESS*'s voice*] Sally Banner was one of my girls
who went on to university. Many of my old girls came back to see
me. I waited but she didn't come back. When France fell I cried
before my class. Not one of them understood why.

[SISTER ROSA*'s voice*] Atheist, pacifist, communist, blasphemer, she
whored her youth away and there was no peace in our time.

[CANON*'s voice*] I will give her a reference, because, as far as I
know, she is a clean-living Christian girl.

> *The* HEADMISTRESS *and the* CANON *come from behind their
> masks as* MOTHER *and* FATHER *and go to the front of the rostrums.
> An* ABC INTERVIEWER *enters with a microphone.*

INTERVIEWER: And everyone's talking about Sally Banner's grand slam:
first, second and third in the Jindyworobak Poetry Competition. Mrs
Banner, I believe Sally was wild—er, a live-wire in her university
days?

MOTHER: Well, no more than most really. They were unsettling times.
The Americans were here, lacing our daughters' milk shakes
with Spanish Fly. It turned their heads. We all worried about our
daughters. What decent mother wouldn't? [*Aside*] She was a real
trollop. She'd lie down anywhere and do it like a dog. It was as if
she wanted to punish us for something. Why, what had we done?
We'd only loved her and protected her.

FATHER: Stopped her from making a fool of herself.

INTERVIEWER: You must be a very proud father, Mr Banner?

FATHER: They said she had talent. I don't know. I never read poetry myself. Highbrow sort of stuff. I don't know where she got it from. Nothing like that in my family. I like a good Edgar Wallace yarn. She had big ambitions, wanted to get away, but the War came. I said: 'Better to be a big frog in a small puddle, Sal'. We didn't see eye-to-eye on much.

The INTERVIEWER *exits.*

BOYS *and* GIRLS *jitterbug in frenzied fashion.* SALLY *and two male partners dance with erotic undertones. One dancer moves left, the other moves right.* SALLY *is left jitterbugging alone.*

Meanwhile, FATHER *continues, aside:*

Understand her! I'd seen bitches like her on heat during the War, but it's rough when it's your own. Man-mad. Couldn't keep her pants on. She had it in for us, ever since I bashed that young bastard's skull in with a lump of four-be-two.

MOTHER: After all we'd done for her.

FATHER: In the morning I'd come down to breakfast. How are you, Sal? Great day?

MOTHER: Good morning, darling. Rise and shine.

SALLY: The world tastes like blood in my mouth.

FATHER: How do you deal with that?

MOTHER: She was sick, that's what I said. Better get her straight to a doctor.

A PSYCHOLOGIST *enters. He holds up a series of inkblot tests.*

PSYCHOLOGIST: Sally Banner, take an inkblot test.

SALLY: [*still dancing*] I see a vagina ringed with decayed teeth.

Laughter.

PSYCHOLOGIST: Very interesting, dear.

SALLY: I see a penis studded with six-inch nails.

Laughter.

PSYCHOLOGIST: Fascinating, dear.

SALLY: I see an avenue of black bums copulating in the gloom.

Laughter.

FIRST BOY: The boongs from the Catalina Base have got their airflow mattresses laid out all over the uni lawns. Wonder who they do it with?

SECOND BOY: Sally Banner.

Laughter.

SALLY: I want to be a second Edith Sitwell.

PSYCHOLOGIST: I think you're trying to have us on, dear.

SALLY: I'll be greater than Sarah Bernhardt.

PSYCHOLOGIST: [*to parents*] All adolescents go through a period of role-taking. The only cure is time. Try to be patient. Never admit how shocked you are.

The PSYCHOLOGIST *exits.*

Music comes up for the DANCERS.

MOTHER *comes downstage and confronts* SALLY.

The music fades.

MOTHER: I smelt semen on your pants last night, Sally.

SALLY: I believe strongly in the blood, the flesh, as being wiser than the intellect.

MOTHER: Hot baths morning and midnight just to bring it on. What a wicked waste!

SALLY: [*hands over her ears*] We can go wrong in our minds, but what our blood feels and believes and says is always true.

MOTHER: *The Tropic of Cancer,* Chesterfields and contraceptives. I took a look in your locker.

SALLY *flees across the stage.*

SALLY: All I want is to answer to my blood direct.

SALLY *removes her shoe and shies it at* MOTHER, *who screams.*

MOTHER: Daddy, Daddy, look what she's doing now.

FATHER: I'll answer you, you bitch.

He shakes SALLY.

Whore, dirty whore.

SALLY *slaps his face. They stand confronting each other, aghast.*

SALLY: I'm going now… with a copy of D. H. Lawrence and a spare pair of pants.

SALLY *moves far downstage. She lies down, placing a raincoat under her head.*

FATHER: Let her go. She'll come home when she's hungry.

MOTHER: Sally, Sally, don't leave us. Come home, darling.

FATHER: Even a genius has to eat.

FATHER *returns upstage.*

MOTHER: You don't have to be ashamed of us anymore, darling. 'Autumn Fires' and 'Bluebell Wood' are out in the lumber room. Van Gogh's 'Sunflowers' are on the picture rail and we don't have autumn tonings anymore.

MOTHER *returns upstage.*

Music rises and the dancing continues.

DAVID, *a university student in his early twenties, emerges from behind* SISTER ROSA'*s mask.*

The music begins to fade.

DAVID: It was a rainy autumn when I found Sally Banner asleep in the men's common room. She lay on her white raincoat with her long, wet hair spread out to dry. She always looked terrible with wet hair. But at that moment I fell in love with her.

He crosses to SALLY *and strokes her sleeping face.* SALLY *stirs, opening her eyes.*

Don't be frightened, it's only me.

SALLY: Who's me?

DAVID: David. I'm one of your silent admirers.

SALLY: I've noticed you giving me the eye.

DAVID: I've watched you for months, walking with your long hair swinging in the light.

SALLY: And heard the dirty mouths after me.

DAVID: Heard that too.

SALLY: Doesn't that make a difference?

DAVID: I don't want to be like the rest. Nobody's loved you. Nobody's understood you.

SALLY: If only I could reach past your body to you.

DAVID: I want to love your mind, your intellect.

SALLY: Lie down beside me, David. The watchman will never find us if we're quiet.

DAVID *stands looking down at her. He covers her with his coat.*

DAVID: [*awkwardly*] You can't stay here forever.

SALLY: I'll think about that later on. Come down and put your arms around me.

DAVID: I can't love you.

SALLY: Take your bloody coat then. I might contaminate it.

DAVID: I'll lie beside you, that's all.

SALLY: Holy, holy.

DAVID: [*kneeling down*] Where are all the others now who had you under the pines on the football oval? Or on the golf links after the golfers went home?

SALLY: They've gone.

DAVID: And all you've got is me.

SALLY: With promises.

DAVID: With some promises.

SALLY: With love.

DAVID: With my kind of love.

SALLY *lies in his arms. He lights cigarettes, giving her one.*

SALLY: Where will I go tomorrow?

DAVID: Tomorrow you'll go home.

SALLY: They'll murder me.

DAVID: Tomorrow you'll go home and this time it will be all right because I'll be there to look after you. I'll ask permission to call.

SALLY: Will you really?

They giggle.

DAVID: And I'll lend you Havelock Ellis on *The Psychology of Sex*. We'll do this thing properly or not at all.

Long pause. He sits smoking.

SALLY: David, I don't think I need to read *The Psychology of Sex*.

DAVID: But I do.

DAVID *moves across to* FATHER *and* MOTHER.

Two GIRL STUDENTS *enter—typical 1940 girls swinging shoulder bags.*

Background music.

FIRST GIRL: She slept with him all night in the men's common room.

SECOND GIRL: She's a nympho. I bet she can't count them on the fingers of two hands.

FIRST GIRL: I often wonder what it really feels like.

SECOND GIRL: Mmm.

She smiles.

FIRST GIRL: Oh! You didn't? You wouldn't...

SECOND GIRL: Tex was very gentle. He says he'll send for me when he gets back to the States... after he gets his divorce. [*She rummages in her bag, and brings out a large photo of Tex.*] He looks divine in his uniform.

FIRST GIRL: Divine!

SECOND GIRL: I only go out with officers. Mummy says they're safer.

FIRST GIRL: How did you feel the first time?

An air-raid siren and the noise of planes. They all crouch down.

SECOND GIRL: [*shouting*] He took me to the Palace and there was blood all over the bottom sheet next morning.

FIRST GIRL: What did you do?

SECOND GIRL: I hid the sheet in the bedside cabinet and sat up and had eggs and bacon on a silver tray. Mummy would have died.

FIRST GIRL: [*sighing*] You're so sophisticated.

The noise increases overhead.

SECOND GIRL: Wouldn't it be awful if it was the real thing this time?

FIRST GIRL: What would you do if the Japs came?

SECOND GIRL: Lie back and enjoy it.

FIRST GIRL: It's okay for you. You've got nothing to lose, baby.

They giggle. Sirens blow the all clear.

The GIRLS *go right and left to dance with* BOYS. SALLY *joins in.* MOTHER *watches anxiously.*

The music rises and fades. FATHER *takes* DAVID *aside.*

FATHER: This book, *The Psychology of Sex.* Do you think it's the right kind of book to lend a young lady?

DAVID: I think all scientific information should be available.

FATHER: With all the various sexual positions marked in red ink?

DAVID: I am a biologist, Mr Banner.

FATHER: Your interest is purely clinical.

DAVID: Impurely clinical.

FATHER: But, good God, there's positions here I've never even dreamed of.

DAVID: Would you like to borrow it for an extra week, Mr Banner?

MOTHER: I really think you're fond of her, David. Truly fond. Not just taking advantage like the others. I really do think he's fond of her.

Pop music. Two GIRLS *and two* BOYS *dance to the front of the stage. The music fades but they continue dancing.* SALLY *jitterbugs by herself.*

FIRST GIRL: She's cheating on him. Everybody knows about it.

FIRST BOY: I gave her a bunch of dandelions yesterday. She took them and smiled. She's a goddess.

SECOND BOY: She's the university bike.

FIRST BOY: She wears her hair like a coat of armour.

SECOND GIRL: She doesn't wear any pants.

SECOND BOY: And walks barefooted in the rain.

DAVID: Last summer we drank crème de menthe in the bar of the OBH. Will we ever see another summer like that again?

> Walking in the rain in winter
> And in summer drinking by the sea,
> Grudge me not then this somewhat,
> For no one knows as well as I how small it is.

SALLY: [*calling*] David. Come on, David.

She dances towards him.

DAVID: Sally, I've been called up.

Pause.

SALLY: Come back soon, darling.

DAVID: Marry me.

SALLY: I don't believe in marriage. I'm going to live with the man I love, and both of us will be free forever.

DAVID: Darling, there's no such thing.

SALLY: Would we have single beds in separate rooms? Sit up and quote poetry to each other all night? What would we do, David?

DAVID: When we married—

SALLY: You'd put Havelock Ellis into practice at last. I don't want a textbook husband.

DAVID: Just an animal.

SALLY: Who wants to love a mind? Minds are too difficult. Nobody can love a mind. But bodies are simple and clean and straight. I know what to do with a body.

DAVID: So I'd noticed.

SALLY: I don't really want anything to change. I want it just as it is, always.

DAVID: Our intellectual romance.

SALLY: It satisfies… part of me.

DAVID: Yes, with all your lovers on the side. The game's over, Sally.

SALLY: You made the rules.

DAVID: I didn't want to be like all the others. I wanted you to think of me differently.

SALLY: You're incapable of love. Or daring.

DAVID: No, I'm a naturally celibate man. And you're a hot-pants. It's an unequal contest.

SALLY: Who'll love my mind now?

DAVID: It'll atrophy for lack of use.

SALLY: I'll meet you by the pool in the courtyard at midnight.

DAVID: Stop playing games, Sally.

SALLY: Will you be there?

DAVID: Last chance.

CHORUS: [*singing*] In the sweet bye and bye
    You'll get pie in the sky when you die.
    In the sweet bye and bye
    You'll get pie in the sky
    When you die.

DAVID *puts on a greatcoat and comes downstage. He stamps his feet to keep warm and smokes.* SALLY *comes up behind him, puts her arms around his waist and lays her head on his shoulder.*

SALLY: David. Guess what? I'll marry you.

DAVID: No you won't.

SALLY: But I said: I'll marry you.

DAVID: And I changed my mind.

SALLY: It was all a lot of bloody talk, then. No love, no promises.

DAVID: You convinced me. You're a very convincing talker, Sally.

SALLY: So I'm naked. Again.

DAVID: Human beings can't bear very much nakedness. It's rather unattractive.

SALLY: I'm naked now. Will you make love to me?

DAVID: Here and now?

SALLY: Yes, here and now.

DAVID: You set hard tasks for chivalric lovers, don't you? The grass is wet. Lie on my coat. Always the gentleman. [*Pause.*] You've lain down here a lot of times?

SALLY: A lot of times.

DAVID: But never for me.

SALLY: This is the last card in my pack.

DAVID: Are you quite sure you want to play it?

> *She pulls him down. They kiss and embrace.*

I can't see your eyes. It's too dark. Is it the green light, Sally?

SALLY: Yes, David.

> *He gets up awkwardly and looks down at her.*

DAVID: Sorry, I'm no good tonight. Never any good to you. And it's fatal to apologise. Get one of your healthy brutes. One of your blind animals. They'll satisfy you. I'm a cold fish.

> *He kneels and places his hand on the grass.*

A small, warm hollow in the grass. All that's left of us.

> *He gets up and pats her thigh.*

Poor little bitch.

> *He walks back to the dais behind* SISTER ROSA*'s mask.*

SALLY: David! David, don't leave me. I can't stand it. Not again. David. [*Getting up on her knees*] David. [*Screaming*] You shit, you rotten impotent shit. You can't do it to me. You can't do it. You *shit!*

MOTHER: I'll make him marry you. Who does he think he is? Lived over a grocer's shop. He won't do this to you, darling.

FATHER: I never liked that book. Havelock Ellis. All those positions marked in red ink. Some I'd never heard of. And I was an Anzac. Something fishy about it.

MOTHER: I'll make a scandal.

FATHER: Something fishy about him.

MOTHER: If she wants him she can have him. She can have anything she wants.

FATHER: Gets on my nerves. Weeping around the house all day. Hasn't she any pride?

MOTHER: He won't get away with this. Sue him for breach of promise.

SALLY: Who am I? Who… am… I?

MOTHER: He ought to be proud to marry you.

FATHER: Pull yourself together.

SALLY: I'm Sally Banner.

MOTHER: All the boys you've had.

SALLY: Who *am I*?

FATHER: You ought to be ashamed.

SALLY: I'm *Sally Banner*!

MOTHER: Offer him a couple of hundred, Daddy. What's money for if it's not to make our children happy?

SALLY: I'm *nobody*!

> *She takes a bottle from the altar, swallows its contents and falls, grabbing her throat.*

MOTHER: [*running to* SALLY] Sally, Sally, what have you done? What's she done, Daddy? She's swallowed lysol. Just like the heroine in *The Way of the Eagle* by Ethel M. Dell.

> *She sticks her fingers down* SALLY*'s throat and forces her to her knees.* SALLY *gags and chokes.*

She's tried to kill herself, Daddy. Oh, the wicked girl. God will punish you. Spit it up. Nothing but trouble. What have I done to deserve it?

FATHER: For God's sake, you're choking her.

> *He pushes* MOTHER *away.*

MOTHER: God is watching you.

> FATHER *takes* SALLY *in his arms and starts shaking her body.*

FATHER: My little girl. You didn't take it, did you? It was just a mistake. You didn't take it, Sally. Sally, darling, tell me you didn't take it.

> *An ambulance siren screams.*

> *The* CHORUS *trundles on a hospital bed.* FATHER *lays* SALLY *on it, then goes back to his original position in front of the rostrum.*

> *During this action the* CHORUS *speaks together and severally.*

CHORUS: What's she done?
  Swallowed lysol.
  She in trouble?
  Burnt her throat out.
  Waistline's thicker!
  On purpose?
  Don't read labels.

  They snicker.

  Pull the other one.
AUTHORITATIVE VOICES: Stand back. Don't touch 'er. Don't crowd 'er.
  Give 'er air.

  Enter two DOCTORS *and two* NURSES, *with a stomach pump, salt and water. They arrange the stomach pump and line up in front of the bed.*

CHORUS: What they doin'?
  Salt an' water.
  She in trouble?
  Pump 'er stomach.
  Give 'er air. Give 'er air. Give 'er air.
FIRST NURSE: That's right, dear, swallow it down.
FIRST DOCTOR: Swallow it down!
SECOND NURSE: Keep it down, dear.
SECOND DOCTOR: Keep it down!
FIRST NURSE: That's lovely, dear.
CHORUS Lovely, dear… that's lovely… lovely…. lovely.

  The NURSES *and* DOCTORS *exit.* SALLY *is left lying motionless on the bed.*

  Swelling ABC radio music. An ANNOUNCER *enters with a live microphone and* MISS FUNT, *an ABC poetry reader.*

ANNOUNCER: This is our Happy Hospital Half-Hour. And a spot of culture today for you lucky people. Miss Sissy Funt will now read the winning entry in the ABC poetry competition, 'Testament', by our local poetess, Miss Sally Banner.
MISS FUNT: [*into the microphone*]
  These have I lost, being too much beloved
  And having for their beauty only this:

That I have loved them.
That cold, white wanton with the stiff-necked pride
Of centuries of narrow-minded squires
Migrating to a strange dark brutal country—

ANNOUNCER: Thank you, Miss Funt.

MISS FUNT: The passion for the land, to feel the soil
Ache through their thin loins, it was like—

ANNOUNCER: [*grappling with her for the microphone*] Miss Funt...
Thank you!

> *He moves across to* SALLY *on the bed.*

Miss Banner, do you think that your childhood in Widgiemooltha tended to give you this sensitivity towards the mysterious solitude of the Australian bush?

SALLY: I think so. I always felt its essential hostility.

ANNOUNCER: You got it, Miss Banner.

MISS FUNT: [*desperately*] Another man's hunger for a wanton woman.

ANNOUNCER: [*icily*] It gives an even more dreadful effect when you speak it than when I first read it, Miss Funt. And while we're with these shocking poems, Miss Banner, I expect you've found that Perth too has come in for its share of war upheaval and change?

SALLY: Oh yes, the War in Perth was a blacked-out city with an evacuating population.

> *Pause.*

ANNOUNCER: And during the War what have you been doing?

SALLY: The intellect is only a bit and bridle. What do I care about knowledge? All I want is to answer to my blood direct without fribbling intervention of mind or moral or what not.

ANNOUNCER: Bravo, Miss Banner. That's the cry that's echoing round the world. That was your young poetess, Sally Banner, a young lady of many talents, at present confined to Ward Two with a throat infection. Cheerio, Miss Banner! I'm sure Widgiemooltha is proud of their little girl tonight.

> *The* ANNOUNCER *and* MISS FUNT *exit.*

> *'Roll Out the Barrel' can be heard.*

> *A* POLICEWOMAN *enters, coming downstage to stand beside* SALLY*'s bed.*

POLICEWOMAN: Sally Banner, pay attention. On the fourteenth day of August, 1945, by mistake did take lysol from a bottle carelessly left unlabelled on a shelf. Sally Banner, to do away with yourself is a punishable criminal offence. Sally Banner, everything to live for. All your life before you. Next time you do it you won't get away with it.

The POLICEWOMAN *exits.*

FATHER: She seems so small lying there. I keep asking myself, what did we do? What did she want?

He staggers and falls.

MOTHER: We've got her where we want her now. Thank God she's safe at last. Daddy, did you hear me? It's an ill wind and whatever is, is best. Daddy? Daddy? What's the matter, Daddy? Daddy. Oh! You wicked girl. You've killed our Daddy.

'The Dead March'. A muffled drum beat.

PALLBEARERS *wearing RSL badges enter with a coffin. They drop red paper poppies on the coffin. The procession covers* FATHER*'s exit.*

PALLBEARERS: [*intoning*]
They shall not grow old, as we that are left grow old.
Age shall not weary them, nor the years contemn.
At the going down of the sun and in the morning
We shall remember them.

MOTHER *weeps.*

A bugle plays 'The Last Post'.

The CANON *enters.*

CANON: [*hastily*] For as much as it has pleased Almighty God in his great mercy to take unto himself the soul of our dear brother here departed, we therefore commit his body to the ground, earth to earth, ashes to ashes and two quid please.

He thrusts out his hand. MOTHER *pays and exits weeping behind the* PALLBEARERS *carrying the coffin.*

Muffled drums in the background.

PALLBEARERS: [*intoning*]

They went with songs to battle, they were young,
Straight of limb, true of eye, steady and aglow.
They were staunch to the end against odds uncounted,
They fell with their faces to the foe.
They mingle not with their laughing comrades again;
They sit no more at familiar tables at home;
They have no lot in our labour of the daytime;
They sleep beyond the foam.

CHORUS: [*singing and circling the stage in a slow parade*]
Sleep my love and peace attend thee
All through the night.
Guardian angels God will lend thee
All through the night.
Soft and drowsy hours are creeping,
Hill and dale in slumber sleeping,
Love alone his watch is keeping,
All through the night.
Though I roam a minstrel lonely
All through the night,
My true harp shall praise thee only,
All through the night.
Love's young dream, alas, is over.
Yet my strains of love shall hover
Near the presence of my lover,
All through the night.

The CHORUS *exits. Voices are heard on the amplifier.*

CANON: Sally Banner, come down out of the chapel tower.
SISTER ROSA: It's peace in our time.
CANON: You'll catch your death.
SISTER ROSA: And raspberry cordial for afternoon tea.
HEADMISTRESS: You have too much natural ability.
FATHER: Big frog in a small puddle.
ECHO: Big frog… big frog… big frog…
MOTHER: Sue him for breach of promise.
SCHOOLGIRLS: [*singing*] Come live with me and be my love.
MAN: You're a dangerous sort of woman, darling.
MICHAEL: It's hard to find a girl who'll do it.

MOTHER: She's at it again.

VOICES: Guilty, Your Honour.

DAVID: Where are all the others now?

MICHAEL: I'm randy and I'm going to the war.

SCHOOLGIRLS: [*singing*] Bring me my Bow of burning gold…

DAVID: They had you under the pines on the football oval.

SCHOOLGIRLS: [*singing*] Bring me my Arrows of desire…

JUDITH: You'll survive, Sally.

VOICES: Sally Banner cracked the mica and lost her virginity.

JUDITH: Walking naked.

VOICES: Guilty, Your Honour. Guilty, Your Honour. Guilty.

CHAMBERLAIN: Now God bless you all. It is the evil that we shall be fighting…

SISTER ROSA: Sally Banner will go straight to hell.

DAVID: Poor little bitch.

CHAMBERLAIN: Brute force, bad faith, injustice, oppression, persecution.

ALL: The communion of saints, the forgiveness of sins and life everlasting.

SALLY: Guilty, Your Honour. Guilty, Your Honour. Guilty.

> SALLY *rises from the bed and comes out on to the apron of the stage.* THOMAS *emerges from the darkness. He is a slight, gentle replica of* FATHER, *dressed in an AIF uniform. He carries a bunch of dandelions.*

THOMAS: I gave Sally Banner a bunch of dandelions in the spring before I went away to war. She took them and smiled. She was a goddess. [*He comes downstage.*] It's Thomas, Sally. You remember Thomas?

SALLY: [*without turning*] Doubting Thomas?

THOMAS: Believing Thomas. I've come to save you, Sally. Repeat after me: I believe in Marxism-Leninism.

SALLY: I believe in Marxism-Leninism.

THOMAS: The dictatorship of the proletariat.

SALLY: The dictatorship of the proletariat.

THOMAS: To serve the working people.

SALLY: To serve the working people.

THOMAS: And promote the cause of peace.

SALLY: And promote the cause of peace.

THOMAS: I believe in bureaucratic, democratic centralism, in reprimand, suppression, suspension, expulsion and the payment of dues.

SALLY: Save me, Thomas.

THOMAS: When the War is over we could get married.

SALLY: Marry me now.

THOMAS: I'm going back to Darwin in the morning.

SALLY: We could get a special licence.

THOMAS: I'll have to ask my mother.

SALLY: I'll wait for you in my red dress underneath the Town Hall clock.

> SALLY *exits.*

> BOYS *and* GIRLS *march in, singing. The* CHORUS LEADER *swings a marching-girl baton.*

CHORUS: Arise, ye workers from your slumbers,
 Arise, ye prisoners of want,
 For reason in revolt now thunders,
 And at last comes the age of cant.
 So away with all superstition,
 Servile masses arise, arise,
 We'll end for e'er the old conditions
 And scorn the dust to win the prize.

> *A clock strikes.*

> SALLY *enters in red dress and red veil.*

THOMAS: Mother says I can't marry you, Sally. It would break her heart. She's taking me on a world cruise after the war.

SALLY: Poor bloody Thomas.

THOMAS: Forgive me, Sally.

SALLY: Goodbye, Thomas.

THOMAS: You were my goddess. You wore your hair like shining armour, but you were the university bike. You failed French three times but they said you were hot stuff in bed.

SALLY: I'm all alone, Thomas.

THOMAS: I've never been to bed with a woman. I'll get a special licence. I won't tell my mother and we'll spend our honeymoon at the Hotel Bohemia.

Hand-in-hand, they walk downstage and kneel centre stage.

Music plays: 'Here Comes The Bride'.

MOTHER, *in a hat, and the* CHORUS *of girls and boys follows the bridal party.*

AMPLIFIER: [CANON*'s voice*] Dearly beloved, we are gathered here as a remedy against sin and to avoid fornication. If either of you know of any impediment why you may not be lawfully joined…

SALLY: [*aside*] I can see your dark head against the winter sky and your throat with the blue shirt and the boy's body. Oh, Jude, why were you a woman?

AMPLIFIER: [CANON*'s voice*] When the secrets of the heart shall be disclosed.

THOMAS: [*aside*] Forgive me, Mother, for I know not what I do.

SALLY: Wait for me by the wattle tree on the river bank. I'll come. If it takes years, Michael, I'll come.

AMPLIFIER: [CANON*'s voice*] Speak now!

SALLY: [*aside*] I don't believe in marriage, David. I'm going to live with the man I love and both of us will be free forever.

THOMAS: [*aside*] Christ! Mother, I cut my umbilical cord.

AMPLIFIER: [CANON*'s voice*] In the name of the Father and of the Son and of the Holy Ghost.

SALLY: I take thee, Thomas.

THOMAS: With this ring I thee wed,
  With my body I thee worship.

MOTHER: I wish her father had been alive to see it.

MOTHER *takes out a handkerchief. All throw confetti over* SALLY *and* THOMAS. MOTHER *weeps.* DANCERS *come forward, chairing* SALLY *and* THOMAS *back to bed.*

CHORUS: [*singing*] It was on the good ship Venus,
  By Christ you should have seen us,
  The figurehead was a moll in bed,
  And the mast was a raging penis.
  'Twas on a China station,
  We caused a great sensation,
  We sunk a junk in a sea of spunk
  By mutual masturbation.

The cabin boy was Kipper,
He was a naughty nipper,
He stuffed his arse with broken glass,
And circumcised the skipper.
The captain had a daughter,
She fell into the water,
Delighted squeals revealed that eels
Had found her sexual quarter.
Oh it's friggin' in the riggin',
It's friggin' in the riggin',
It's friggin' in the riggin',
And there's fuck all else to do.

They throw SALLY *and* THOMAS *onto the bed and dance around in a ring.* THOMAS, *in army issue woollen underpants, is drunk, holding on to bed head.* SALLY *is crouched on the end of the bed, crying, stripped to bra and panties.*

THOMAS: I can't do it, Sally darling. I can't consummate our conjugal rights. [*Touching her awkwardly*] Piss off, you bastards. Sally and I can't consummate our conjugal rights.

Laughter. Figures dance and drink in dim light.

CHORUS: [*singing*] Poor Sally, she never made it,
Not even suicide.
When she swallowed lysol they gave her salt and water.
So she never died.

MOTHER: [*coming to the bed*] Sally, Sally, here's your wedding present: a copy of Marie Stopes and a Dutch cap.

Laughter. MOTHER *returns to her mask.*

CHORUS: Poor Sally, she married Thomas,
They tried and tried and tried.
In the honeymoon suite of the Hotel Bohemia
They lay down and cried.

THOMAS: Sally, Sally, after the War we're going to change the world.

Laughter, cheers, catcalls, confetti, singing 'Friggin' in the Riggin''.

SALLY *is wheeled offstage on the bed like a victim on a triumphal chariot.*

THOMAS *goes back to his mask and dons his* CANON*'s robes. He is joined by the* HEADMISTRESS *and* SISTER ROSA. *They all pray.*

CANON: Our Father…

SISTER ROSA: Which art in heaven…

HEADMISTRESS: Hallowed be Thy name.

CANON: Thy kingdom come…

SISTER ROSA: Thy will be done…

HEADMISTRESS. On earth as it is in heaven

BOYS *and* GIRLS *march ceremonially around the stage singing with the* AUTHORITY FIGURES, *'Land of Hope and Glory'.*

ALL: Land of hope and glory,
Mother of the free,
How can we extol thee
Who are born of thee?
Wider still and wider
Shall thy bounds be set.
God who made thee mighty,
Make thee mightier yet.
God who made thee mighty,
Make thee mightier yet.

HEADMISTRESS: VJ Day, and nearly thirty thousand throng the streets.

CANON: Pageantry, prayers and thanksgiving mark an inspiriting ceremony.

SISTER ROSA: Most of the revellers are young, and some irresponsible.

HEADMISTRESS: The fire brigade has received ten false alarms.

A fire alarm, laughter.

SISTER ROSA: And the ambulance two false alarms.

An ambulance siren turns into an air-raid siren. The siren stops, the noise of planes is heard overhead. The crowd freezes. All look up.

AUTHORITY FIGURES: A one, a two, a three…

ALL: [*singing and dancing*]
Put your left foot in,
Put your left foot out,
Put your left foot in
And shake it all about.

AUTHORITY FIGURES:
>   We'll do the hokey pokey
>   And we'll turn right around,
>   That's what it's all about.

CANON: By two o'clock, the famine and exhaustion from parading the streets led to an orgy of kissing.

SISTER ROSA: Which far exceeded the bounds of common decency.

HEADMISTRESS: Some windows were smashed in the city and, in all, excessive revelry led to the arrest of thirty people.

AUTHORITY FIGURES: A one, a two, a three…

CHORUS: [*growing lewd*]
>   Put your backside in,
>   Put your backside out,
>   Put your backside in,
>   And shake it all about,
>   We'll do the hokey pokey and we'll turn right around.

AUTHORITY FIGURES: That's what it's all about.

> *A bomb goes off. The dancers freeze, looking up.*

CANON: Japan has surrendered.

HEADMISTRESS: Surrendered to our every demand.

SISTER ROSA: The last of our enemies has been laid low.

> *Cheers, whistles.*

AUTHORITY FIGURES: A one, a two, a three…

ALL: Put your front in,
>   Put your front out,
>   Put your front in,
>   And wiggle it about.
>   We'll do the hokey pokey
>   And we'll turn right around.

AUTHORITY FIGURES: That's what it's all about.

CANON: To lay healing hands upon the tortured peoples at the cost of a few explosions seems a miracle of deliverance.

HEADMISTRESS: The clear light of democracy shines on into years of peace.

SISTER ROSA: And the wildflowers of Hiroshima bloom more avidly than ever before.

ALL: [*chanting*] Morning glory, day lilies, hairy fruit bean, sesame, purslane, clotsbur, Spanish bayonets, goosefoot.

CANON: We are concerned with doing a job.

ALL: [*chanting*] Morning glory, day lilies, hairy fruit bean, sesame, purslane, clotsbur, Spanish bayonets, goosefoot, panic bean and fever few, the bells of St Bartholomew.

HEADMISTRESS: The dropping of the bomb was done by military men under military orders.

SISTER ROSA: We are supposed to carry out orders, not question them.

CHORUS: [*circling and singing*]

This is the way we wash our hands, wash our hands, wash our hands,

This is the way we wash our hands, bitter cold in the morning.

Morning glory, day lilies, hairy fruit bean, sesame, purslane, clotsbur, Spanish bayonets, goosefoot.

The CHORUS *changes the game, chanting.*

Panic bean and fever few
The bells of St Bartholomew.
When shall I pay you,
Tomorrow or the next day,
Chippety chop, chippety chop...

They continue to chant and play the game. Finally they circle around the last figure, SALLY BANNER, *then part to make way for* MICHAEL, *who imprisons her.*

MICHAEL: The last man's head, head, head, is *off*!

The dancers run offstage, laughing. The AUTHORITY FIGURES *retire behind their masks.*

Hallo, Sally.

SALLY: Hallo, Michael.

MICHAEL: I heard you got married.

SALLY: Eight months ago.

MICHAEL: I didn't think you would.

SALLY: Didn't you?

MICHAEL: I thought I'd always be able to come back and find you.

SALLY: And take up where you left off?

MICHAEL: I guess so.

SALLY: There I'd be waiting patiently whenever you decided to arrive.

Two years? Three years? Come off it, Michael.

MICHAEL: You've changed, grown hard-hearted.

SALLY: Six lovers, one attempted suicide, one wedding later, is that surprising? How did you find out I was married?

MICHAEL: My parents wrote: 'Sally got married the other day'.

SALLY: And how did you feel then?

MICHAEL: I just felt shocked. It was impossible. You couldn't belong to anyone else but me.

> *He sits beside her.*

But after a few days I could see that this was stupid. You didn't belong to me. You belonged to yourself. I had no rights.

SALLY: You did. You did have a right.

MICHAEL: Well, I forfeited it, then. So I thought: 'I'll always be grateful to Sally. She taught me about women. She—'

SALLY: Oh, for Christ's sake.

> *They laugh. He takes a bottle out of his greatcoat pocket. They take turns drinking.*

How was I to know you ever thought of me?

MICHAEL: Who did you marry?

SALLY: I married Thomas: good, loving, clever Thomas. Oh, he's very amusing and kind.

MICHAEL: But you don't want goodness and kindness.

SALLY: No.

MICHAEL: You never did. It's no use blaming me, Sally. You got what you asked for.

SALLY: Did I?

MICHAEL: And you're still asking.

SALLY: Yes, Michael.

> *She leans against his shoulder. They drink again. He kisses her.*

MICHAEL: Let's get out of here. Let's go down to the beach.

SALLY: It's two o'clock in the morning.

MICHAEL: Does it matter?

SALLY: No.

MICHAEL: Why do you always go for broke, Sal?

SALLY: I don't play for halves. I take it all the way.

MICHAEL: There can't be any good come out of it. You know that?

SALLY: You said we had nothing to do with goodness or kindness.

MICHAEL: We'll destroy each other.

SALLY: Destruction? Well, perhaps that's the only way I'll get my wish.

> MICHAEL *and* SALLY *cross the stage hand-in-hand, smoking. He puts his greatcoat halfway around her.*
>
> *'Night and Day' plays.*
>
> *A* MAN *enters, one of the comic-sad wanderers of any city in the early morning. He takes chalk from pocket and lovingly prints on the altar: 'eternity'. He stands back to admire it, then exits.*
>
> MICHAEL *and* SALLY, *in pale, light lie down on his greatcoat.* MICHAEL *throws away his cigarette.*

MICHAEL: Come up close and keep out the cold.

> SALLY *moves into his arms.*

SALLY: What will happen to us?

MICHAEL: I don't care what happens. This is a bonus.

SALLY: I can remember it forever.

MICHAEL: I could always remember the shape of your face. I could draw it like a heart in the dark. And yet there'd be times when I wouldn't remember you at all. And suddenly, you'd be up and betray me. You were a bitch, the things you'd do to me.

SALLY: What things?

MICHAEL: There was this Canadian nurse. I was in bed with her. You're jealous?

SALLY: Yes.

MICHAEL: I had all her clothes off. She was lovely, and suddenly I said, 'I love you, Sally,' just like that. It was fatal. She froze. 'Who's this Sally?' she said, getting dressed. So I told her. 'You'll go back home and marry her after the War,' she said. 'No,' I said, 'Sally and I weren't geared for marriage.'

SALLY: I thought if I tore you out of me I'd be deformed in some way. I'd need plastic surgery. So after you left I lay down anywhere for practically anyone who asked me. I wanted to destroy myself, because I didn't exist anymore. Not as a whole, loving, complete human being.

Pause.

MICHAEL: [*angrily*] You didn't do that, did you? Lie down for everyone?

SALLY: You can't bear it, can you?

MICHAEL: No.

SALLY: You'll get used to it, and when you do it will make it easier for you to tell me to lie down for you. Then when you leave me again you'll think: 'She's already a moll. I can't corrupt her.'

MICHAEL: [*kissing her*] You're a cruel bitch.

SALLY: Do you know the morning after I married Thomas I woke in that hotel bedroom pounding the pillows crying: 'Michael, Michael'? It was wicked of me to marry Thomas, because it went against my nature and I knew it. I used him and that was inexcusable, because he's a much better person than you are. He's a friend. But there's something morally wrong with my being married to him. It's much more moral for me to be here with you than in bed with Thomas.

MICHAEL: When's Thomas due home?

SALLY: A month, two months.

MICHAEL: Come closer then, Sally. Not much time left. [*Kissing her*] Your skin smells of salt.

Pause.

SALLY: Every time the surf falls on the beach I think this is forever, and every time the tide sucks it back again I know we're lost, we've got no future and never can have.

'Begin the Beguine' starts to play.

BOYS and GIRLS enter, throwing streamers to a departing ship.

BOYS & GIRLS: Ta-ta, don't forget to write. Have a good trip. Ta-ta, Mum. Goodbye, Dadda. Be a good girl. Don't do anything I wouldn't do. Take your seasick pills. Aussies forever.

Music: 'The Star Spangled Banner'.

A spotlight picks up a GIRL sitting on a suitcase, weeping. The ANNOUNCER enters with portable microphone.

ANNOUNCER: And it's a great day down at the wharf, folks, as the first US bride ship pulls away, leaving the wharf literally littered with streamers, Coke and mothers' tears. The American invasion is over and there they go—the pride of Aussie, hundreds of our girls, the sweethearts of Australia chasing the Yanks down the shipping lanes to San Francisco.

San Francisco open your golden gates,
You'll let no stranger wait,
Outside your door…

But what's this? Somebody's been left behind, folks. This little lady has missed the bus—or should I say ship. [*He gives a forced laugh.*] Here's a human interest story for you. Her name is…

He thrusts the microphone into the GIRL*'s face.*

GIRL: [*sobbing*] Micky Snatchit.

ANNOUNCER: Well, Miss… er… Snatchit. [*Eyebrows raised to the audience*] What's your story?

GIRL: I couldn't make it, I just couldn't make it.

ANNOUNCER: Never mind, love. Catch the next one.

GIRL: [*howling*] I love Chuckie but I couldn't leave Mum.

ANNOUNCER: Another human tragedy of the War, folks. And with the sound of her tears ringing in our ears we say farewell to Micky Sn—er, Micky. Say farewell to the folks, Micky, and a cheerio for Mum waiting at home.

GIRL: Farewell. [*In a storm of sobs*] Cheerio, Mum. Oh, Mum, I couldn't make it.

ANNOUNCER: And top of the charts today and especially for you is 'Wish Me Luck'. Take it away, boys.

Music plays.

The ANNOUNCER *and* GIRL *exit.*

The scene returns to SALLY *and* MICHAEL *lying on his greatcoat.*

SALLY: Mike, I'm going to have a baby.

MICHAEL: [*jerking upright*] You're kidding!

SALLY: It's true.

MICHAEL: How do you know? You've never had a baby before.

SALLY: I've missed two periods and I'm sick every morning.

MICHAEL: Shit! [*He rises, moves away, and lights a cigarette.*] You'll have to find… someone. [*He throws away the cigarette in rage.*] The luck, the rotten bloody luck. And Thomas due home any time. A few more days and I'd—

SALLY: You'd have been out of it.

MICHAEL: I didn't say that. Oh! We thought we were so sophisticated, didn't we? The rules didn't apply to us. Well, we got ours. [*Pause.*] It makes the whole thing so bloody... cheap. My father used to watch the girl on the verandah opposite with her boyfriend. He was always laying bets about when she'd get knocked up. And sure enough, there she was with her belly up. I can hear him laughing now. Just the way he'll laugh at us.

SALLY: Your father. Who gives a stuff for your father? God rot all fathers with the dirty little greasetraps they call minds.

MICHAEL: That girl had her baby. She kept it. I always thought she was game.

SALLY: Is that what you want?

MICHAEL: It's up to you, isn't it? [*Pause.*] You're on your own, Sally. I thought you knew that.

> SALLY *gets up slowly. They stand looking at each other. He turns away.*

Get in touch with me when you've found a doctor. [*Moving upstage*] It's a shame. Our kid... it would have been really something. What do they call them? Love children.

> *He looks at her. She sinks down centre stage.*

But you can't break the rules, Sal.

> *He moves far upstage into darkness.*

SALLY: [*reciting, with musical accompaniment*]
Did you besiege Helen's Troy
And take her with the glittering gold
And brush of eyelashes on the singing wind?
Light the match in Troy
That sets the burning love in Helen's eyes
Naked before the host.
Release death, sings the wind,
Release death...

AMPLIFIER: Relax, dear. That's it. Re-lax. Good girl. Have you got the money? Many thanks. Pay before delivery.

> *Hearty laughter.*

Dim lights.

MICHAEL *is still upstage, his back turned to* SALLY.

MICHAEL: Sally, are you all right?

SALLY: Yes.

MICHAEL: I'll leave you, then. Better if we're not seen together. [*Long pause.*] No use prolonging the agony.

He walks off, wooden faced.

SALLY: Let the marriage with your carnal beauty
    Be consummated in the hush of evening,
    What price but the love in Helen's mouth,
    Leaving no breath on mirrors.
    Troy perishes.
    The thin cylindrical towers,
    Mist-dropped, vanish,
    As Helen stood once, shading her eyes,
    Late in the summer for your return.
    No reason left for her to wait,
    For the bright brief kiss of you, Boy,
    Let Helen's limbs grow hard and cold,
    Inviolate in Troy.

MOTHER: [*coming from behind her mask*] Is that you, Sally? Sally, why don't you answer me?

The conversation is conducted at a distance.

SALLY: Yes, Mother.

MOTHER: I haven't set eyes on you for months. How can you neglect your own flesh and blood like this? Sally, are you listening?

SALLY: I'm listening, Mother.

MOTHER: Home isn't really home anymore. Since Dad died there's nothing left for me. I only wish I could join him.

SALLY: Yes, Mother.

MOTHER: My life's over.

Silence.

Sally, what's the matter with you? Is anything wrong? Sally, answer me this instant. Is anything wrong?

SALLY: Nothing, Mother.

MOTHER: I think you ought to know, people are talking. You've been seen with a man. Have you been seen with a man? Honestly, I don't even know why I try. It's your reputation. But you're such a fool. You wouldn't consider how careful you've got to be now. You know how people talk. Although I've always said, there's no smoke without a fire. Sally?

SALLY: I'm here, Mother.

MOTHER: You haven't been… seeing anyone, have you?

SALLY: I'm all alone.

MOTHER: That's good, darling.

> THOMAS *enters from behind the* CANON*'s mask, carrying a bunch of dandelions. He comes downstage to* SALLY.

THOMAS: Sally, Sally darling.

SALLY: Yes, Thomas.

THOMAS: Are you feeling better, darling?

SALLY: I don't think I'll die this time. Did they tell you what was wrong with me?

THOMAS: No, but it doesn't matter now.

SALLY: Cowards! Well, I'll tell you. I've been aborted. You've been in Darwin for twelve months so it obviously wasn't yours.

THOMAS: Whose was it, then?

SALLY: Michael's. Remember I told you once about Michael?

THOMAS: The bastard.

SALLY: No. Not a bastard.

THOMAS: Cuckolded, Sally. Cuckolded, by God.

> *He laughs rather wildly and throws down the dandelions.*

SALLY: My baby's dead, Thomas. I've killed my baby. [*Holding out her arms to him*] Forgive me. I couldn't help it. I wanted some kind of immortality.

THOMAS: [*taking her in his arms*] Sssh, darling. Ssh, darling. It'll be all right. I'm here, Sally. Don't cry. It's not worth crying so hard about it.

SALLY: It is worth it. It's got to be.

THOMAS: [*moving centre stage*] No, quite worthless, Sally. The things that matter aren't our own little egos, our happiness, our satisfactions. The things that matter are building a new shining life for everyone.

In five years we'll have socialism. And you and I will have helped
to build it. That's our immortality.

SALLY: I'm not good enough, Thomas.

THOMAS: You're better than anyone. Braver and stronger and better
than anyone I know.

SALLY: Am I, Thomas? I wanted to go back to the golden age. Primitive,
savage, beautiful. I wanted to be free.

> *They stand with arms around each other. Vera Lynn singing
> 'There'll Be Bluebirds Over the White Cliffs of Dover' comes
> over the amplifier.*

HEADMISTRESS: Freedom. The bells of history are chiming out *our*
song. We are living in great days, through historical years and hearts
are swelling with hopes of future peace.

SISTER ROSA: The alternatives were never so clearly posed. Good
against evil, might is right, the Cold War and God on our side.

> *The* CHORUS *of boys and girls enters, marching, carrying red
> flags and banners. They march around and around* SALLY *and*
> THOMAS *in a circle, singing 'The Red Flag'.*

CHORUS: [*singing*] The workers' flag is deepest red,
  It shrouded oft our martyred dead;
  And 'ere their limbs grew stiff and cold
  Their life blood dyed its every fold.
  Then raise the scarlet standard high.

> *They chair* SALLY *and* THOMAS *around the stage.*

  Beneath its folds we'll live and die,
  Though cowards flinch and traitors jeer,
  We'll keep the red flag flying here.

> *They begin to march offstage, preferably through the audience,
> still chairing* THOMAS *and* SALLY *in a triumphant procession.
> Their* VOICES *grow fainter as they disappear.*

  Look round, the Frenchman loves its blaze,
  The sturdy German chants its praise,
  In Moscow's vaults its hymns are sung,
  Chicago swells its surging song.
  With heads uncovered, swear we all

To bear it onward 'til we fall.
Come dungeons dark or gallows grim
This song shall be our parting hymn.

END OF ACT ONE

♦ ♦ ♦ ♦ ♦ ♦ ♦ ♦

ACT TWO

The stage is very brightly lit. The AUTHORITY FIGURES *are in place. Carnival music is belting out. Large signs advertise 'The Haunted Horror House', 'The Tunnel of Love', 'Bubbles and Her Famous Shower Bath', 'The Honolulu Hula Girl'. The director may use grotesque sideshow figures if s/he wishes: large puppet figures or cartoons of the snake-girl, the Polynesian dancer, Bubbles and the Stripper. Two men and a woman are dressed as sideshow spruikers and there are six sideshow girls: a Mexican snake-girl, a hula dancer, a stripper, Bubbles, an Egyptian dancer and a slave girl.*

SALLY BANNER *stands behind the altar, which now serves as a political rostrum.* SAUL, *a Communist organiser, is older than* DAVID. *He wears a hat, but care should be taken not to make him the Bolshevik cartoon.*

The real audience provides the audience for the political speeches. A few voices planted in the auditorium help with the illusion. The atmosphere is confused, tormented, garish.

AUTHORITY FIGURES: [*capering, singing*]
    Come listen all kind friends of ours:
    We want to move a motion,
    To make an eldorado here,
    We've got a bonzer notion.

    A raspberry.

ALL: [*lewdly*] Bump us into Parliament,
    Bounce us any way,
    Bang us into Parliament
    On next election day.

    Raspberry.

HEADMISTRESS: Oh yes, I am a Labor woman
    And believe in revolution;
    The quickest way to bring them on
    Is talking constitution.

Raspberry.

CANON: They say that kids are getting scarce,
         I believe there's something in it.
         By extra laws I'd incubate
         A million kids a minute.

Raspberry.

SISTER ROSA: I've read my Bible ten times through
         And Jesus justifies me,
         The man who does not vote for me,
         By Christ he crucifies me.

Raspberry.

ALL: Bump us into Parliament,
         Bounce us anyway,
         Screw us into Parliament
         On next election day.

Raspberry.

FIRST MALE SPRUIKER: Walk right up and get your tickets now. The only show where it all comes off and it all hangs out. The only show where anything goes. I'll say it's going to be a naughty one this one, I'll say don't miss this one. I'll say this one is going to make your shirt go up and down your back like a venetian blind.

FEMALE SPRUIKER: Hurry, hurry, hurry, hurry to the Haunted Horror House. If you have a weak heart don't enter. Loose articles are not allowed to ride. It's beaut, beaut, beaut to be lost in a maze. It's a little bit daring, it's a little bit naughty, but by golly it goes in nice.

SECOND MALE SPRUIKER: Don't miss the Indian rope trick. I haven't seen anything as straight as that since I was married twenty years ago. At the far end of the line we've got the Mexican snake-girl, we've got a hula dancer from the Polly-neesian islands. When she takes off her clothes it'll make the ol' feller stand up.

FEMALE SPRUIKER: Gather round, gather round, gather round. Who's game enough, man enough, sport enough to dance with the one and only Bubbles? Watch her take her famous shower bath, watch her do the dance of lo-o-ve.

FIRST MALE SPRUIKER: Look at that woman take off her clothes, I don't know why she puts 'em on. She's never in 'em long enough to wear 'em.

SECOND MALE SPRUIKER: You'll be screaming help, help, help, inside the Haunted Horror House. We give you the entertainment you pay for inside the Haunted Horror House.

SALLY: I used to think a man of genius could be excused many things. I know now that a man of genius can be excused far less than any ordinary man.

FIRST INTERJECTOR: We'll excuse you, love.

SECOND INTERJECTOR: She wants to be excused.

Laughter.

FIRST MALE SPRUIKER: Here, here, here she is. Give your chains a rattle, darling. Shake it around a bit, darling. Let's see if it's still alive.

SALLY: My life is an indictment against escapism.

FIRST INTERJECTOR: Escape with me, darling.

SALLY: A man who believes in nothing is an easy dupe for Fascist ideology. I hid my head in the poetic sands 'til world events forced me to pull it out again.

SECOND INTERJECTOR: Pull it out and pull it off, love.

Laughter.

ALL: Bump us into Parliament,
        Grind us anyway,
        Stuff us into Parliament
        On next election day.

FEMALE SPRUIKER: The oldest dance in the world, the dance of the seven veils. C'mon ladies, c'mon gents. Hurry, hurry, hurry.

SALLY: My disbeliefs were the disbeliefs of many of my generation: a painful awareness of the world we lived in, a belief in the irresponsibility of big business, conventional politics and mass education alike...

SECOND MALE SPRUIKER: [*interjecting*] Step inside to the Haunted Horror House. Come 'ere, come 'ere, come 'ere. We want a few more starters...

SALLY: With the fiery quality of complete intellectual honesty and conviction we can expose the role of reaction from the time of Christ to the People's War.

> GIRLS *and* BOYS *walk across the stage carrying slogans: 'Ban the H-Bomb', 'Free Speech', 'Nazism is Dead?', 'Ban the Commos', 'Better Dead than Red', 'War in August', 'Stop World War III', 'Cheaper Vegies', '40 Hours', 'No Crimes Act'. They line up in rival factions.*

FIRST INTERJECTOR: [*singing*] Jesus wants me for a sunbeam.

SECOND INTERJECTOR: Fair go, fair go, give the little lady a go.

SALLY: The complaints of the priests and Pharisees against Christ was exactly the complaint of the great capitalists against us: 'He stirreth up the people.'

FIRST MALE SPRUIKER: Come on, boys and girls, mums and dads and grandmas, put your money on the house, put your money on the Haunted Horror House.

SALLY: Bombay's bazaars run with workers' blood, India's giant millions demand bread and freedom. It is plain that the Soviet Union alone stands for peace, in deeds as well as words. [*Singing*]

> Soviet Land so dear to every toiler,
> Peace and progress walk with thee,
> There's no other land the whole world over
> Where man walks the earth so brave and free.

FIRST INTERJECTOR: Go back to Russia.

SECOND INTERJECTOR: What about Uncle Joe?

SECOND MALE SPRUIKER: She's going to do the striptease absolutely different. She calls it 'Bounce Your Boobies'.

CROWD: [*screaming*] Strip, strip, strip.

> *They advance towards* SALLY; *she retreats.*

> SAUL *enters from behind* SISTER ROSA's *mask. He leaps behind the altar.*

SAUL: [*raising his hand to quieten them*] Australian democrats, for Sally Banner there is no neutrality. She has taken up her position with the working class in their struggle.

FIRST MALE SPRUIKER: They call her the skew-whiff girl, the girl with the rhythmic chest, and when she's finished she's got nothing on but her beautiful smile.

FEMALE SPRUIKER: Hurry, hurry, hurry, hurry, ladies and gents, here they go now, here they go, here they go *now*. Come on, come early, step right up and look at what we've got to offer. Fun and games and an easy win, only two bob a throw and every little bitch helps. All you have to do is throw your balls, throw your balls at the fabulous big mouth of 1948.

The CROWD *begins to pelt the* AUTHORITY FIGURES *with balls. Amplified crowd noises. 'I've Got a Lovely Bunch of Coconuts' is heard.*

FIRST INTERJECTOR: Come on, inter 'em. Put in the boot.

SAUL: Australian democrats, let us fight to put an end to this dangerous foreign policy.

SALLY: The monopolists shelter the war criminals. They cry peace with their fingers itching on the atom bomb.

SALLY and SAUL are pelted. There is a general punch-up. Two POLICEMEN *enter. Silence falls.*

FIRST POLICEMAN: You are charged with addressing a public meeting.

SECOND POLICEMAN: [*chanting*] Without the permission of the Commissioner of Police.

They grab SALLY and SAUL.

SAUL: [*struggling*] We workers vigorously protest at this flouting of democracy and free speech.

SALLY: [*rapidly, as she is frogmarched off*] We demand and will fight for our right to criticise the rotten capitalist system which has only war, depression, high prices, high profits, low wages, slave conditions in a police state to offer the workers.

Laughter, cheers, clapping, boos.

ALL: [*dancing*] Bump us into Parliament,
    Root us anyway,
    Shag us into Parliament
    On next election day.

Raspberry.

FEMALE SPRUIKER: It's a little bit naughty, it's a little bit daring, but by golly it goes in nice.

FIRST MALE SPRUIKER: Pack it in, love. The show's over.

They exit.

The carnival music winds down, as the stage darkens.

SALLY *enters to take up her position in front of the* AUTHORITY FIGURES.

SALLY: I refuse to plead in your court. I know that I certainly won't receive any justice here. I am here because I did rebel and that's the only reason.

HEADMISTRESS: [*stepping out from her mask, sadly*] Sally was always a rebel in thought and deed, and she did not tone with time.

SALLY: I refuse to take any part in helping the ruling caste perpetuate the illusion of justice.

CANON: [*stepping out from his mask*] I'm sure I never gave her a reference. I could find no evidence that she was a clean-living, Christian young woman.

SALLY: Who pays the judges? Who decides what the law will be? For whom is it enforced?

SISTER ROSA: [*entering*] Blasphemer, pacifist, atheist, Communist. She defied God.

SALLY: You own the courts, you are the judges. That is why I defy your courts, that is why I urge anyone who has any dealings with this force to defy it also.

The HEADMISTRESS *puts on an apron and becomes* MOTHER. *She comes downstage.*

MOTHER: [*chanting*] Daddy's rotating in his grave, Sally. You're breaking your mother's heart. We gave you everything you wanted. You only had to ask. Daddy left us comfortable, the rents are coming in and the shares are going up, but you're a dirty Commo, Sally, and you won't get a penny over my dead body.

SALLY: [*chanting*] Keep your shares, keep your houses, I don't need them now, for I'm a dirty Commo, Mother, and I renounce it all.

MOTHER *exits weeping behind the* HEADMISTRESS*'s mask.* SAUL *enters from behind the mask of* SISTER ROSA. *The scene is played in a spotlight.*

SAUL: You were very brave today, Sally. I was proud of you. You've got a fine future ahead in the Party.

SALLY: I'm a poet not a politician.

SAUL: Poets are tuppence a dozen. I can make you a good organiser, Sally.

SALLY: Can you, Saul?

SAUL: You think I'm conning you, don't you? That because you're a pretty girl I can't keep my hands off you, you in your tight skirts and little lacey blouses, and you're dead right.

He bends over the altar and kisses her passionately.

It'll be the end of me in the Party if you give me away. You always struck me as the sort of girl who'd tell her husband.

SALLY: I am. Are you afraid?

SAUL: Bloody afraid, because if it came to a choice between you and the Party you know what I'd choose, don't you?

SALLY: Yes, your wife. Don't leave me, Saul.

SAUL: You've got Thomas and a child.

SALLY: That's what I thought I wanted; but you're exciting. I love your darkness and your Jewishness and your... authority. I guess I'm looking for a hero, Saul. And you're a hero. You fought in Spain.

SAUL: If you could have seen us: a rabble, crawling with lice, our bellies empty, running towards the sea.

SALLY: All right, you failed, but you fought for something you believed in.

SAUL: Stop idolising me. I don't want to be any silly little bourgeois girl's Party pin-up. Look, Sally, don't you mess me about. If there's to be anything at all, it's got to be on my terms. And when I say finish, it's finished.

She reaches up, pulls his head down and kisses him.

THOMAS *comes from behind the* CANON *'s mask, pushing a baby's pram downstage.*

THOMAS: Sally... Sally...

SAUL: [*whispering*] You stay and I'll go out the back way quietly. Oh, I'm a good organiser.

SAUL *moves upstage behind* SISTER ROSA *'s mask.*

THOMAS: Is that you, Sally?

SALLY: Yes, Thomas.

THOMAS: You're awfully late. Was there any trouble?

SALLY: Some trouble.

THOMAS: You're not hurt, darling?

SALLY: No, of course not, Saul was with me.

THOMAS: Saul's a good man to have in a brawl. Did you make a rousing
    speech?

SALLY: Saul said I did.

THOMAS: He's a marvellous leader, isn't he? Inspiring. I'd follow him
    to hell. [*Pause.*] Sally…?

SALLY: Yes, yes he is… inspiring.

THOMAS: The baby's been crying a bit.

SALLY: Get some sleep. It's late.

THOMAS: Are you coming to bed soon?

SALLY: Soon.

THOMAS: Don't be long, darling. The bed's cold without you.

>   *He moves upstage.* DAVID *moves down from behind* SISTER
>   ROSA'*s mask: older, drunk, in civilian clothes.*

DAVID: Are you there, Sally?

SALLY: Who is it?

DAVID: It's me.

SALLY: Who's me?

DAVID: Your errant old lover, David.

SALLY: Sssh, David. Go away, it's late.

DAVID: Sally… I've come for comfort. Do you know where I've been,
    or care? Not you. I've been drinking for three days. I've forgotten
    time. I've forgotten myself. I've even forgotten you.

SALLY: And you're blaming me. You had your chance. I begged you to
    marry me, and you sent me away. You only ever wanted what you
    couldn't get.

DAVID: A fatal compromiser.

SALLY: You never wanted me, not the fleshly living me, just some
    beautiful abstraction.

DAVID: Hit me, Sally, kick me when I'm down.

THOMAS: [*from upstage*] Sally, who's out there?

SALLY: It's only David, Thomas.

DAVID: Dear maternal Sally, let me sleep on your soft bosom. Rock,
    rock me, rock me…

THOMAS: For Christ's sake, Sally. Piss him off and come to bed.

DAVID: [*laughing*] Piss him off and come to bed. I'd know what to do
    now, I'd know very well what to do.

SALLY: Don't start it up all over again.

DAVID: Kiss me, Sally.

She kisses him.

A motherly goodnight kiss. I won't come back again. I know I've got to get over you, but when I'm drunk my feet fly to you like a homing pigeon.

SALLY: There's nothing I can do anymore.

DAVID: Sure, Sal, sure I'll stagger out into another dawn, marry a nice girl, forget you. Does that make you jealous?

SALLY: Yes.

DAVID: Ah, Sal, Sal, you bitch, you unmitigated bitch. You want us all, don't you? Sally Banner's harem. Well, you can't have us. It's bigamy, my love. Go rock your baby.

He staggers upstage behind SISTER ROSA's *mask.*

THOMAS: Sally, has David gone yet or will I throw him out?

SALLY: He's gone, Thomas. David's gone.

She pushes the pram with her foot and begins to sing 'Atomic Lullaby'.

Hush my baby do not cry,
The mushroom cloud is in the sky;
Now I lay you down to die,
Lulla lulla lullaby.
Hush my baby do not cry,
A mother's tears are never dry;
If you should die before I wake,
I pray the Lord your soul to take.
But who will heal my bitter ache?
Lulla lulla lullaby.
Hush my baby do not cry,
A mother's tears are never dry.

Two BOYS *and two* GIRLS *enter talking, smoking.* SALLY *pushes the baby's pram centre stage. She takes a bundle of papers from the foot of the pram.*

FIRST GIRL: It's Sally Banner. She came to a bad end and joined the Commos. Hasn't she gone off?

SECOND GIRL: Pretend you don't see her.

They turn their backs.

Cheeky thing.

SALLY *thrusts a paper into their faces.*

SALLY: *Star, Workers' Star.* 'Cold War Hots Up'.

FIRST GIRL: Is that you, Sally? Fancy that being you. Ooh! You have changed.

SECOND GIRL: No, thank you!

She tears the paper into bits. The GIRLS *exit.*

FIRST BOY: Hey! It's Sally Banner. Hot pants Sal. Why doncha go home and get married?

SECOND BOY: How'd ya like to be shacked up with that?

BOTH: Like a bit, Sal?

Laughter. The BOYS *exit.* MICHAEL *enters.*

SALLY: *Workers' Star.* Rally for Peace and Freedom.

MICHAEL: [*softly*] Sally.

She swings around.

I can draw the shape of your face in the dark. Like a heart. And yet there've been times when I couldn't remember…

SALLY: And that was most of the time.

MICHAEL: It was no use prolonging the agony.

SALLY: Is that what you called it?

MICHAEL: Sally, what did you want, what did you really want?

SALLY: I wanted you to say: 'I love you. Have our baby and we'll go away together'. But you didn't say it, did you?

MICHAEL: If it's any satisfaction, I've missed you.

SALLY: Except when you forgot my face.

MICHAEL: Did you ever think of me?

SALLY: When I saw our baby lying there, a lump of bloody gristle, I thought of you, and I hated you.

Pause.

MICHAEL: [*recovering*] And now you're happy?

SALLY: I had Thomas's baby to replace the one we murdered. And I speak on soap boxes but I never write poetry anymore. It's as if I'd turned dumb forever.

MICHAEL *moves towards her.*

Stay where you are.

MICHAEL: [*triumphant*] You're afraid, afraid I'll touch you.

He laughs. She closes her eyes.

Go home then, go home to Thomas. Feed your baby, carry your banner, sweet Sister Sally. and never see me again.

Her eyes fly open.

Where's my brave wild girl gone now?

SALLY: You destroyed her.

MICHAEL: She's indestructible, and she wants me still.

SALLY: No.

MICHAEL: What if I was to say I've learnt my lesson, that every girl in every bed was you, every corner I turned in every crummy town I hoped you might be there?

SALLY: Leave me alone, Michael. Please.

MICHAEL: I'll wait for you tonight under the bridge. You'll come. I know you, Sally.

He leans closer, careful not to touch her. She stands rigid. He drops a coin in her hand.

Give us a *Workers' Star.* Funny, you never struck me as a likely recruit to the ranks of the working class, Sal.

He moves upstage, whistling, and sits on the altar.

SAUL *comes from behind* SISTER ROSA*'s mask, and takes up a position on the far right of the stage.* THOMAS *comes from behind* CANON*'s mask and takes up his position on the far left.* SALLY *stands centre stage with the pram.* MOTHER *comes from behind the* HEADMISTRESS*'s mask below the rostrum. The impression is of* SALLY *as the focus of many pairs of accusing and demanding eyes.*

The lights dim.

SALLY: The earth upon its axis turns,
Season on season all delights renew,
But still the sweet delight I find in you
Is old as rain and fresh as morning dew,
Because there is a loveliness that burns,
That burns so tenderly between us two.

Ours is a strong, an earthly loveliness,
I see myself in you, yourself in me,
We love and hate ourselves most tenderly;
Lover to lover lost in fierce caress,
Such contradictions mock mortality.

Thomas, Thomas, I've written another poem at last.

THOMAS: Who did you write it for, Sally?

SALLY: For myself.

SAUL: Sally. [*She swings around.*] My spies tell me you've been seen with another man?

SALLY: You said we had no future. No second places for me, Saul.

SAUL: You're a randy little bourgeois bitch. The only thing that interests you is what you've got between your legs.

MICHAEL: Choose, Sally, choose.

THOMAS: You slept in the spare room last night, Sally. I didn't even hear you come in.

SALLY: Thomas…

THOMAS: Saul, I don't know what to do. She's seeing this man. They had a boy and girl affair years ago. She seems to have gone mad.

SAUL: It's up to you, Thomas. Deliver an ultimatum, or close your eyes and wait 'til she gets over it.

MOTHER: That child's neglected, Thomas. You ought to put your foot down. Sally needs guidance. Let her see who's master.

MICHAEL: Choose, Sally, choose.

THOMAS: Sally, don't lie to me. You're such a bad liar. It shows in your eyes.

SALLY: I lie because I can't bear to cause you so much pain.

THOMAS: And cause me twice as much.

SALLY. Forgive me, Thomas, I want him. I can't lose him again.

THOMAS: And all we've built together, it's all to go for nothing?

MICHAEL: Choose, Sally, choose.

SALLY: All I know is I'm happy when I'm with him and miserable when we're apart.

THOMAS: Happiness, what's happiness? Why is happiness so important?

SALLY: What else is there?

THOMAS: We are quite different, aren't we? We haven't really got anything in common.

MICHAEL: Choose, Sally, choose.

MOTHER: She needs horsewhipping. To leave that poor little child like that and a good husband.

THOMAS: Saul had the right idea. Saul warned me.

SALLY: You discussed our private affairs with Saul?

THOMAS: I have the greatest respect and admiration for Saul.

SALLY: Thomas! I've been having an affair with Saul for months.

> *Pause.*

THOMAS: You don't leave me with anything, do you? Marriage, friendship, good faith, it's all a dirty lie. And you're what they told me you were, a whore.

SALLY: If you say so.

THOMAS: But you won't get your hands on our child. I'll fight you for custody in every court in the country.

SALLY: Michael told me you'd use blackmail but I wouldn't believe him.

THOMAS: The bastard. He gets me whichever way I go. Leave me then, leave me with nothing. Take the lot—Michael, the child, happiness.

MICHAEL: Choose, Sally, choose.

THOMAS: But how will I forget your little pendant breasts and your funny, soft legs?

SALLY: Goodbye, Thomas. You keep the baby.

> *She pushes the pram towards him.*

THOMAS: You're not fit to be a mother.

SALLY: Be happy, Thomas. Doubting Thomas. [*Pause.*] But what will I do without you? Who'll look after me?

MICHAEL: I'll look after you, Sally.

> *He jumps down from the altar.*

MOTHER: [*coming downstage*] Three thousand in cash to keep away from my daughter.

MICHAEL: Three thousand! Make a real offer, Mrs B. Is that all she's worth? Your only child?

MOTHER: Three thousand pounds is not to be sneezed at.

SAUL: Sally, I *am* jealous.

SALLY: I know.

SAUL: You know too bloody much. Don't go or I'll have to break you.

SALLY: I'm leaving, Saul.

SAUL: You're finished. You know that? Politically, you're finished.

SALLY: I'm in love with him. I always have been.

SAUL: Love, what's love? Sex. I can't understand your language. Keep him as a sexual object, if you can be discreet about it.

SALLY: You're disgusting.

SAUL: But of course you have no discretion: politically unreliable, your career in the Party finished. I'm almost sorry for you, Sally.

SALLY: No, I'm sorry for you, Saul. I'm sorry for all of you. Love, joy, honesty—they're just words to you. You're cowards. Afraid of life. Life's not an abstraction. It's not a set of rules or a great sacrifice of the self. It's all we've got, and I'm going to live it to the fullest stretch of my imagination. And you're going to die. I choose Michael.

> *She moves into* MICHAEL's *arms. A* CHORUS *of boys and girls enters, bringing on the bed.* SALLY *and* MICHAEL *lie on the bed together as the* CHORUS *sings and dances 'Sally Go Round the Moon'.*

CHORUS: Sally fed me bananas,
Chocolate roughs in the sun;
I had a whirl with a Luna Park girl,
Took off her clothes one by one.
Sally go round the moon, Sally,
Sally go round the sun.
Tossed them over a windmill,
She wore her luminous smile,
Mirrored like Lady Godiva
In my watch with the luminous dial.
Sally go round the moon, Sally,
Sally go round the sun.
As cockcrow broke this morning,
Before she woke she smiled.
She kissed me once, she whispered:
'The Queen of Hearts is wild.'
Sally go round the moon, Sally,
Sally go round the sun.

We cannot stop its motion,
But we can make time run.
Sally feed me bananas,
Chocolate roughs in the sun.
Sally go round the moon, Sally,
Sally go round the sun.

AMPLIFIER: [VOICES *of* CANON, HEADMISTRESS, SISTER ROSA *in an echo-chamber*] Sally… Sally… Sally. God is watching you. God is watching you, Sally… Sally… Sally…

The CHORUS *crouches far right.*

[CANON*'s voice, chanting*] There's something nasty waiting in the woodshed…

[HEADMISTRESS*'s voice, chanting*] Some seed is swelling in the womb of time…

[SISTER ROSA*'s voice, chanting*] By the pricking in my thumbs, something wicked this way comes…

[*All three*] Sally… Sally… Sally…

MOTHER *comes from behind the* HEADMISTRESS*'s mask.*

MOTHER: Your baby's dead, Sally.

SALLY, *stunned, moves centre stage.*

SISTER ROSA: [*coming out from her mask*] Put the screens around the bed.

CANON: [*coming out from his mask*] God's will be done.

MOTHER: We reap what we sow.

MICHAEL: [*from the bed, putting out his hand*] Sally—

SALLY: Don't touch me. I don't want anyone to touch me.

SALLY *crouches centre stage.*

SISTER ROSA, CANON, MOTHER & CHORUS: [*together, singing*]
'M' is for the million things she gave me,
'O' because she's growing old,
'T' is for the tears she shed to save me.

SALLY *puts her hands over her ears.*

'H' is for her heart of purest gold.
'E' is for her eyes with love-light shining,
'R' is right and right she'll always be.

Put them all together they spell 'Mother'.
Mother means the whole wide world to me.

ALL: Happy Mother's Day, Sally!

SALLY: O little children of the earth
I had a child to sing
So sweetly that the birds were quiet
Even though it was spring.
O little children of the earth,
I cry out in my pain,
Give back the lovely wings of birds,
The soft sting of the rain.
Feathers and snow and flying birds,
All things that children know
Destroyed forever and the rain
Drops bitter sweet and slow.
Drops bitter sweet and dreadful
Falling on field and town,
Hiroshima, Hiroshima,
Now we all fall down.

The CHORUS *of girls and boys marches, sings, dances, then groups on the far right of the stage.*

SALLY *rises, joining the singers and leading them in song.*

MICHAEL *rises from bed, puts on overalls and takes a gladstone bag. He moves far left, puts on a welding mask and begins to mime welding.*

CHORUS & SALLY: [*together*]
We got to ban the H-Bomb
'Cause, brothers, after all,
Who wants to be a pile of ash
Or a shadow on a wall?
Or a shadow on a wall.

FIRST GIRL: Six hundred million have signed for peace.

FIRST BOY: One hundred and thirty-four thousand Australians ban the bomb.

SALLY: It's a question for the whole human race, a plebiscite all over our planet. Not crowns and thrones, not war ministers and chancellories, but the Berts and the Bills, the Gladyses and the Janes. They are the decisive force in the struggle for peace.

GIRL: [*shouting*] Broken Hill for peace.

ALL: [*chanting*] People's China, three hundred and forty-three million; Japan, three hundred and thirty-nine million; Soviet Union, one hundred and seventeen million; Korea, seventy million; Vietnam, one million, four hundred thousand.

BOY: [*shouting*] Everybody signed in Mahoney's shearing shed.

GIRL: Nobody signed in Widgiemooltha.

SALLY: I am playing the game of life against death. I am a peace monger, I sign with the millions: thou shalt not kill...

> MICHAEL *ironically breaks in, juxtaposing his song, 'Overtime Rock'.*

MICHAEL: [*singing*] Sleeptime, worktime, overtime rock,
Sleeptime, worktime, overtime rock.

CHORUS: [*softly, dancing like somnambulists*]
Sleeptime, worktime, overtime rock,
Sleeptime, worktime, overtime rock.

MICHAEL: What about playtime? Ain't no play, jus'
Sleeptime, worktime, overtime rock.

> *The music becomes stronger, and the dances wilder.*

> MICHAEL *does a rock-beat solo in front of the* CHORUS,

That's what they call me, the Overtime King,
Brain bees abuzzin', ear bells ring.

CHORUS: Shala-laala.

MICHAEL: Went to the boss, I said, 'What's the score?
Wages buy nothin', can't live no more.'
He says, 'Ha-hu-ha you're a lucky free man,
Free to work all the overtime you can.'
Well...

CHORUS: Overtime, overtime, overtime rock,
Yeah! Overtime stagger 'n rock.
We'll have some overtime, overtime, overtime rock,
Overtime, overtime, overtime rock,
Overtime, overtime, O, O, overtime,
Staggerin', staggerin', stag, stag, staggerin',

Overtime staggers, overtime staggers,
Overtime stagger 'n *rock.*

MICHAEL: Can't stand no more of that overtime rock—yeah!

MICHAEL collapses onto the bed during the last lines of the song. The BOYS *and* GIRLS *exit.*

The lights dim.

MICHAEL lies asleep with legs flung out. SALLY *comes to the bed and looks down on him. She sits beside him, taking up a trailing hand.*

SALLY: Mike.

Silence.

Mike. Wake up.

MICHAEL: [*groaning*] Whassup? Whassa matter? Ah, go to sleep, for Chrissake. What you wake me up for? Shit, I'm tired.

He turns over and SALLY *stands up.*

SALLY: You're always tired.

MICHAEL: I know what you want.

SALLY: No you don't.

MICHAEL: [*watching from the bed*] You want to use me up.

SALLY: You never look at me anymore.

MICHAEL: Eat me alive.

SALLY: I've forgotten what it's like to be loved. [*She tries to get into bed.*] Shift over.

MICHAEL: Why should I?

SALLY: I want to sleep with you.

MICHAEL: You make me feel like a stud bull.

He shifts over. She lies beside him, bending over him.

SALLY: Don't you still love me?

MICHAEL: You don't want a man. You want some idolised fucking machine.

SALLY: You don't want me anymore?

MICHAEL: Not much.

She jumps up and moves away.

SALLY: What do you want?

MICHAEL: I've got... conservative tastes. I'm a plain, uncomplicated man and I like my women virtuous. It's as simple as that.

SALLY: It's got to be worth it. I've strewn the world with wreckage to get to you. Make it work, Mike.

MICHAEL: Relax, Sal. It's not studded with diamonds. You think you can heal the world with that great compassionate cunt of yours but you're not one of the great whores of history. You're a de facto, living in a pokey bed-sit in the suburbs.

SALLY: [*coming to him*] Let's get married. Maybe then I'll feel more secure.

MICHAEL: [*sitting on the edge of the bed*] Marry you, an amateur moll like you? Marry a crow who deserted her husband and kid!

SALLY: How dare *you* say that to me?

MICHAEL: [*getting up*] Ah! Shut up or I'll give you a clip on the bloody ear.

SALLY: What a prize bastard you turned out to be.

MICHAEL: You think you deserve something better?

SALLY: And I thought you were wonderful: wild and strong and great. You've destroyed everything, and you've done it without a tear. It's all gone. [*She puts out her hand.*] Where did it go, Mike? Where did it all go?

> MICHAEL *stands with tears on his face. She notices them at last.*

Michael. You're crying. Don't cry. It's not so bad really.

> *She puts an arm around him.*

Why are you crying?

MICHAEL: [*turning away*] Life's hard, Sal. Life's so hard.

> *He exits.*

> *The* CHORUS *enters.* SALLY *sits on the bed, the* CHORUS *circling around her.*

CHORUS: [*singing*] Sally, Sally,
Marry me, Sally,
And happy forever I'll be,
When skies are blue you're beguiling
And when they're grey you're still smiling, smiling,
Sally, Sally, marry me, Sally,
You're more than the whole world to me.

The CHORUS *exits.*

MICHAEL *enters, with lighted incinerator.*

SALLY: [*softly*] Marry me, Michael.

MICHAEL *pushes her off the bed.*

MICHAEL: [*laughing*] Sally, my dear de facto Sally, always ready, always able. What's known as a good root.

He goes to the bed and begins pulling manuscripts out of mattress.

SALLY: [*sprawled on the floor*] What do you think you're doing?

He takes papers to the incinerator and burns them.

MICHAEL: I'm burning your poems, burning your lies about me, burning you. You filthy bitch with your filthy lies!
[*Reading*] 'And so our love is constant as the storm,
All grief lies lonely in your brief embrace.'
Brief is fucking well right. Burn you bastard, burn.

He throws it in.

SALLY: 'Then must I carry Jackstraw all my days,
The humpbacked victim of a childish sin?
How far? How far? And the voice answers me:
As far as love you'll carry him.'

MICHAEL: Lies, all bloody lies. I'm burning your bloody lies.

He takes armfuls of papers and throws them into the incinerator.
SALLY *gets up slowly and moves towards the auditorium. She does not look back but leaves him with the fire. He does not notice her go. She moves up the aisle.*

The CHORUS *enters.*

CHORUS: [*singing*] Come live with me and be my love,
And we will all the pleasures prove,
Of peace and plenty, bed and board,
That chance employment may afford.

BOYS: I'll handle dainties on the docks.

GIRLS: And thou shalt read of summer frocks,

CHORUS: At evening by the sour canals
We'll hope to hear some madrigals,

If these delights thy mind may move,

They repeat as if the needle on a record were sticking.

Come live with me, live with me, live with me…

SALLY: [*from the auditorium*] Out of the night that covers me,
Black as the pit from pole to pole,
I thank whatever gods may be,
For my unconquerable soul.

SALLY *exits. Laughter from all.*

CHORUS: [*singing*] Sally go round the moon, Sally,
Sally go round the sun.

Music: 'Let's All Dance the Polka'.

Let's all dance the polka,
With Stalin and Gomulka,
Stuff your wig up your thingamejig,
Arse up with care.
Sold me soul for brandy,
And rode outback with Andy,
Flogged me ol' wig for twenty quid,
Stuff all the nation.
Jiggerup, pokerup,
Way down in Widgiemooltha,
I'm mounted on the squatter's wife
One, two, three, sir.
Let's all dance the polka
With Stalin and Gomulka,
Stuff your wig up your thingamejig,
Arse up with care.

The CHORUS *exits, pushing off the bed and singing 'Let's All Dance the Polka'.* MICHAEL *exits.*

The CANON, HEADMISTRESS, SISTER ROSA *enter, singing and dancing the polka around the stage. The* CHORUS *re-enters wearing black cloaks. They dance the polka and sing.*

The AUTHORITY FIGURES *take their places behind the altar. The* CANON *pounds the bench with a gavel. They all pound with gavels. The* CHORUS *takes up positions around the courtroom.*

CANON: Order in the court.

HEADMISTRESS, CANON, SISTER ROSA: [*taking a syllable each in rotation*] We de-clare this Roy-al Com-mis-sion o-pen and we call— [*In unison*] Who do we call?

CHORUS: Who do they call? Who do they call? [*Whispering*] Sally Banner... Sally Banner. Who? [*In a loud roar*] Sally Banner!

VOICES: [*from around the theatre*] Sally Banner... Sally Banner... Sally Banner...

> The CHORUS *sings 'Let's All Dance the Polka'.*

> SALLY *enters, led by two* POLICEMEN. *She moves as if sleepwalking. She is led before the altar as if to a witness box. The* POLICEMEN *take up a position below the altar.*

HEADMISTRESS: Sally Banner, what would your parents think?

CANON: Look out for number one, that's my advice.

> *He bangs his gavel.*

SISTER ROSA: Sally Banner, you are charged that on the fourth day of the fifth month at six o'clock in the afternoon—

CANON: On June fifth, 1949, you met a man in a brown hat carrying a black briefcase.

HEADMISTRESS: I thought she had a rendezvous in the Botanic Gardens at six o'clock on an afternoon in June under Governor Phillip's statue.

SISTER ROSA: No, no. It was on the sixteenth on the Friday evening at half past seven she met at Queanbeyan in the vicinity of Young's store at eight o'clock at night. There's the receipt.

HEADMISTRESS: Where's the receipt?

CANON: She received two thousand five hundred pounds and regards from Sadovnikov.

HEADMISTRESS: *And* Pakmananov.

SISTER ROSA: She sold her soul for six bottles of brandy—

CANON: And twenty quid.

SALLY: I never.

HEADMISTRESS: You never have?

SALLY: No, never.

CANON: Why not?

HEADMISTRESS: Answer the question.

SISTER ROSA: Surely the Commission should have the support of all loyal Australians?

CANON: No reliance can be placed on her evidence.

SISTER ROSA: She has violently opposed the Commission.

HEADMISTRESS: Do you remember the eighteenth of October?

SISTER ROSA: The twentieth of December?

HEADMISTRESS: The second of January?

CANON: The first of August?

SISTER ROSA: What day of the week was that?

SALLY: That would be Sunday.

CANON: And do you remember the preceding day?

SALLY: Yes, on the Saturday.

HEADMISTRESS: All day?

SALLY: All day.

SISTER ROSA: On the sixteenth?

SALLY: [*exasperated*] On the sixteenth on the Friday evening at half past seven—

CANON: Stop making speeches.

HEADMISTRESS: And answer the question.

CANON: An extraordinary exhibition of truculence, evasion and lying.

ALL: *Guilty. Guilty. Guilty. Guilty.*

> The CANON *bangs his gavel.*

CANON: Order in the court. If there are more demonstrations of this nature I will be delighted.

SALLY: I object.

SISTER ROSA: I object to you.

CANON: Objection sustained.

SALLY: There is no justice.

SISTER ROSA: This is not a court of justice.

HEADMISTRESS: This is a court of law.

CANON: I wish to cross-examine the prisoner.

ALL: Cross-examine the prisoner.

CANON: Are you now or have you ever been a member of any political party?

SISTER ROSA: Did you ever discuss Communism with your sister?

HEADMISTRESS: Do other members of your family share your political views?

CANON: Were you active in the Democratic Rights Council, a shareholder in the People's Publishing and Printing Association?

SISTER ROSA: Did you in fact join the Australian Society for Scientific Research, the Legion of Christian Youth, the Australian Russian Society, the Christian Socialist Movement?

HEADMISTRESS: The Australia-China Society, the Council for Civil Liberties, the Housewives' Association, the Australian Arts Council, Sheepskins for Russia, Soviet House, the Civil Rights Defence League, the Russian Social Club, to disseminate the Communist faith and propaganda?

CANON: Are you a member of the CP, are you sure? When did you cease to be, did you join the CP, in short you joined the CP.

SISTER ROSA: This enquiry must not restrain or suppress freedom of thought.

HEADMISTRESS: This enquiry will not be used maliciously to smear any person's reputation.

The HEADMISTRESS *exits.*

CANON: Did you know of it, what did you know of it? Have you ever been to Marx House?

ALL: *Guilty. Guilty. Guilty.*

CANON: She has a scandalous reputation. In all my years on the bench I have never had a more disgusting, a more depraved, a juicier, dirtier… kiss me, kiss me, kiss me… *kiss me harder.*

He climbs onto altar to get to SALLY.

SISTER ROSA: Hide your eyes, hide your eyes, hide your eyes.

CANON: Ahem! Call the first witness.

The CANON *exits.*

ALL: First witness.

MOTHER: [*coming forward*] Sally, say after me: 'Make the tea, mop up the bloodstains'. Write one hundred times: 'I must not tell lies against my mother'.

ALL: Sally, say after me—

SALLY: I must not tell lies against my mother. I must… I must not— Mother, Mother, a man is exposing himself under the black horse-hair sofa. Mother, Mother, the sun's going down, there's a madman rattling the long French doors in the bedroom, the wind shakes and shakes. The knob comes off in my hand. Mother. *Mother!*

MOTHER: She's got such a remarkable imagination, my Sally.

MOTHER *exits behind her mask.*

SISTER ROSA: Call the second witness.

SISTER ROSA *exits.*

ALL: Second witness.

FATHER: [*coming out from behind the* CANON*'s mask, wearing a long, grey, transparent veil*] Sally, say after me: two and two make four, four and four make nine; God Save the King and forget me not.

SALLY: God save me and forget you not.

FATHER: There's a low bed in the earth for the world's cold. Sally, say after me:

Come through the glass, Sally,
Come through the glass,
Come where the dead blue ladies pass.
Come through the glass, Sally,
Come through the glass.
Remember me, remember me.

He returns to his mask. The HEADMISTRESS *re-enters.*

SALLY: Between the devil and the deep blue sea you lay across my bedroom door, listened for the gnawing mouse, the lusting boy.

HEADMISTRESS: Call the third witness.

ALL: Third witness.

THOMAS: [*coming from behind* CANON*'s mask*] Sally, say after me: I must not commit adultery, I must not desert my child, I must not let it die.

ALL: Sally, say after me…

SALLY: I must not commit adultery, I must not desert my child, I must not… I must not… I must…

THOMAS *goes back behind the mask.*

ALL: What day of the week was that? What day of the week was that?

SALLY: No… No… No…

HEADMISTRESS: The witness shows a distinct inability to remember, or to speak the truth. Call the fourth witness.

ALL: Fourth witness.

SAUL: [*coming from behind* SISTER ROSA'*s mask*] With the events in Poland and Hungary, a number of our members have adopted an anti-Soviet position, an anti-socialist position, an anti-working-class position. I will have none of this thinking.

SALLY: Aggression, invasion, occupation, suppression of freedom—

SAUL: Intervention is merely an academic question, a case of who gets there first. We are not liberals, comrades.

SALLY: I have disobeyed the Party. I have read the text of Khrushchev's speech on Stalinism. Stalin stood for genocide, murder, anti-Semitism, spying, torture, careerism, hypocrisy, bigotry—

SAUL: [*gabbling*] You are expelled from the Communist Party of Australia for conduct violating the rules of the Party, factional and splitting activities, flouting the constitution, refusing to recognise the leadership, ignoring directions, vilifying the Soviet Union and the mass working-class movement for economic gains, unity and peace. [*He puts up his hand to stop interruptions.*] Furthermore, I denounce Sally Banner, minstrel of the grubby bedroom, lover of the seamy side of life, pseudo-revolutionary, ideological leader of intellectual delinquents, decadent, bourgeois, revisionist, factionalist—

> SAUL *has moved back behind* SISTER ROSA'*s mask. The* CANON *re-enters.*

SALLY: I make my own pattern.

ALL: [*laughing*] Martyr, saint.

SALLY: I believe in the brotherhood of man. I am a citizen of the world.

CANON: Sally Banner, citizen of the world, how do you plead?

SALLY: How am I charged?

CANON: Sally Banner, you betrayed the system.

SALLY: Guilty.

ALL: Guilty.

HEADMISTRESS: Sally Banner, you believed in freedom.

SALLY: I did everything I could.

ALL: Sally Banner, you walked naked—

SALLY: 'A condition of complete simplicity costing not less than everything.'

ALL: Guilty.

HEADMISTRESS: Sally Banner, for all our sakes, it is necessary that you be guilty.

ALL: *Guilty. Guilty. Guilty!*

> *The voices are raised higher and higher over the* AUTHORITY FIGURES, *who sing 'Let's All Dance the Polka'.*

> SALLY *steps down and moves centre stage, still very much mistress of the situation. She faces the audience with her back to the* AUTHORITY FIGURES.

SALLY: It matters not how strait the gate,
How charged with punishment the scroll,
I am the master of my fate,
I am the captain of my soul.

> JUDITH *comes from behind the mask of* SISTER ROSA. *She is dressed in grey sisters' robes, and stands grimly on the dais with folded arms.*

JUDITH: It's too easy, Sally.

> SALLY *swings around, shocked.*

SALLY: Jude.

JUDITH: This is the time of justice. I call witness number five.

ALL: Witness number five? Witness number five? Witness number five?

CANON: [*banging his gavel*] Order in the court, order in the court. Recall the prisoner.

> *The* POLICEMEN *bring* SALLY *back to the foot of the altar.*

ALL: Witness number five.

> MICHAEL *enters.*

MICHAEL: Sally Banner, that bitch I lived with. I'm not likely to forget her. Said she loved me. Love? It was herself she was in love with. Didn't give a stuff about me. [*To the audience*] Haven't got the price of a drink on you, have you, dig? Bit short this week. [*Laughing*] Ah well, worth a try, wasn't it? World fit for heroes to live in.

> MICHAEL *exits.*

JUDITH: What were you looking for, Sally?

SALLY: Love. I was looking for love.

JUDITH: You were looking for yourself.

JUDITH & CHORUS: [*together*] Cursed…

JUDITH: … are the arrogant.

ALL: Plead, plead, how do you plead?

SALLY: [*whispering*] Guilty.

JUDITH & CHORUS: [*together*] Cursed…

JUDITH: … is she that perverts the judgement of the stranger.

JUDITH & CHORUS: [*together*] Cursed…

JUDITH: … is she that maketh the blind to go out of their way.

SALLY: I believed it, I believed it all: Russia, the holy city, Jerusalem.

JUDITH: No doubts, no questions.

SALLY: It was sincere… dishonesty.

JUDITH: In this case ignorance was inexcusable.

SALLY: I was innocent.

JUDITH: It is always easier to be innocent.

SALLY: It seemed the way out then, to replace oneself by the world.

JUDITH: To be saved by Thomas?

SALLY: In the public square I forgot… the private virtues.

JUDITH: Creativity, love, warmth, freedom. *You* forgot those?

> SALLY, *downstage centre, speaks to the audience.*

SALLY: It was annihilation. I could never accept annihilation. The shadow of it lay over everything I did. My whole life has been a struggle to be identified with someone, something, anything that gave me even a brief sense of my own immortality. And yet I've always known, even when I struggled hardest, that annihilation was the end of it. Even when—no, especially when—I was wild with joy because I thought I'd found, even for a moment, that immortal otherness at last.

JUDITH: So it was deliberate perversity?

SALLY: It was a deliberate decision.

> *They confront each other.*

ALL: [*gleefully*] How do you plead, how do you plead?

SALLY: Guilty, and I'm back where I began.

JUDITH: Where are your children?

> *Pause.* SALLY, *agitated, strides about the stage.*

SALLY: Both my children are dead.

JUDITH: Why did you destroy them?

SALLY: [*challenging, but despairing*] For a great love.

> The CHORUS COURT MEMBERS *nudge each other, snicker, and rock with laughter.*

ALL: A great love... *a great love!*

JUDITH: What was that great love?

SALLY: Love of myself. You said it. I wanted to live so completely a dozen lives, to suffer everything.

JUDITH: Why?

> *She is moved by* SALLY, *suborned in spite of herself.*

SALLY: [*proudly*] I heard a voice from heaven say unto me: 'Write'.

JUDITH: And what did you do?

SALLY: [*defeated*] I wasted my substance.

JUDITH & CHORUS: [*together*] Cursed...

JUDITH: [*triumphantly*]... is she that perverts the gifts of heaven.

ALL: [*singing*] Poor Sally, she never made it,
> No matter how hard she tried.
> She tried hard not to know it,
> But she was a minor poet
> Until the day she died.

ALL: [*closing in for the kill*] How do you plead? How do you plead?

SALLY: *I walked naked through the world.*

ALL: Guilty!

JUDITH: Very few of my acquaintances ever looked very good naked. Minds seem to be much the same. Those I know who go about being brutally honest without a rag of concession for the outraged reticence of others are a nuisance.

> *All exit except* SALLY.

SALLY: [*singing*] I passed my love on the street today,
> He looked through my head and he looked away.
> When I searched in the dust I could only find
> A man with his lips and his eyes gone blind,
> And all that we were, and all that we knew,
> Has gone with the wry, dry dust that blew.
> O where has he gone. O where has he gone,
> My love on whom the good sun shone?

With an ache in his mouth and a crack in his song,
That golden boy to look upon.
And he'll never come back and I'll die alone,
Flesh of my flesh and bone of my bone.

AMPLIFIER: April fourth, Martin Luther King murdered in Memphis.

SALLY *moves right and sits.*

DAVID *comes from behind* SISTER ROSA's *mask, dressed only in underpants, carrying his trousers. He sits beside* SALLY, *looking ill at ease.*

DAVID: You've got a marvellous set of muscles between your legs, darling.

He turns and puts his arms around her.

That's a job that's needed doing for twenty years. And we did it so well.

SALLY: [*brightly*] Isn't it lucky, David, you caught me between husbands?

DAVID: [*stiffly*] I'm married, Sally.

SALLY: Not successfully.

DAVID: Not very. I drink too much, stay out too late, treat her badly. She only says: 'Oh! Davie, not sloshed again?' [*He mimics cruelly a college accent.*] Hallo, darling. [*Pushing back her hair*] You're still rather beautiful.

SALLY: Stay with me, David. Stay with me tonight.

DAVID: I'm expected home early.

SALLY: I wouldn't ask for much. I'd be the most undemanding mistress. Just reassurances now and again.

DAVID: That's something I can't even give myself.

SALLY: David, that night by the university pool, when you knocked me back. Why did you do it? I've wondered about it for years and now I'm old enough to ask you why.

DAVID: I couldn't get—you're not going to believe this—I couldn't get my army-issue trouser buttons undone. I was a very raw recruit.

SALLY: God, why does everything I do turn into such a farce? Let's start again. Have dinner with me?

DAVID: Please, Sally. We'd only finish up in bed again.

SALLY: It's not the sex. I'd love to be with you.

DAVID *puts on his trousers.*

DAVID: Leave it. I don't want it to get complicated. I'm always very bad on the follow through.

SALLY: David, please.

DAVID: I'm just a shit, Sally, just a cold shit. Put it down to that.

SALLY: I'd warm you.

DAVID: Something that needed doing has been done, an error of omission rectified. And now, goodbye, sweetie. No phone calls, no letters. Is it a bargain, Sally? Don't look back.

SALLY: I might turn into a pillar of salt.

DAVID *moves back behind* SISTER ROSA's *mask.*

AMPLIFIER: August twenty-first, Czechoslovakia invaded.

A nurse pushes MOTHER *onstage in a commode wheelchair.* SALLY *moves forward uncertainly.*

SALLY: It's me, Mother. It's Sally. I've come home for you to look after me. You always wanted me home, Mother.

MOTHER *peers helplessly at* SALLY *from her chair.*

It's Sally, Mum. You remember me? *Sally.* I've come home!

The nurse wheels the chair closer. MOTHER *grips* SALLY's *arm and tries desperately to mouth something, then begins to cry. The nurse stows* MOTHER *in her wheelchair and wheels her behind the mask.*

Mother, it's me, Sally. Sally!

AMPLIFIER: September third, Ho Chi Minh dead.

JUDITH *comes from behind* SISTER ROSA's *mask.*

SALLY: [*turning back, centre stage*] Let me stay with you, Jude. Now we can have a life together.

JUDITH: No.

SALLY: I loved you always, Jude.

JUDITH: I live at the school now. Look!

She spreads her robes.

SALLY: Forever?

JUDITH: Forever.

SALLY: A kind of perpetual Sister Rosa, still demanding that I bow?

JUDITH: Yes.

SALLY: Is it any kind of an answer?

JUDITH: It's a sanctuary.

SALLY: You're safe now, Jude. I can't touch you now. So I took a ride on a roundabout. Close the circle and I end where I began.

JUDITH: You make every post a suffering winner, don't you, Sally?

SALLY: So is that all there is in the end, to accept oneself, to be finally and irrevocably responsible for oneself? Jude, I wanted to find in this dirty, scheming, contemptible world something, some kind of miraculous insight… [*To the audience*] I had a tremendous world in my head and more than three-quarters of it will be buried with me.

> *Pause.*

> JUDITH *moves back to her mask.* SALLY *moves to the far left of the stage.*

> DANCING BOYS *and* GIRLS *enter, 1970s style, chanting: 'Peace Now, Peace Now, Peace Now' to Cat Stevens' 'It's a Wild World'. The stage is full of dancing, stomping figures.*

> SALLY *stands isolated, watching them.*

> *The roar of planes, police sirens.*

> *The music fades and the dancers freeze.*

AMPLIFIER: September twentieth, Luna Ten soft-lands on the Sea of Fertility; and Sally Banner, OBE, flies home by Qantas.

> *The scene dissolves into an airport reception. The* CHORUS *and* AUTHORITY FIGURES *crowd around* SALLY *with imaginary microphones and notebooks.*

CHORUS: What are your plans for the future?

SALLY: Cremation.

> *The* CHORUS *begins to disperse.*

JUDITH: Sally Banner, what is your opinion of full-frontal nudity?

SALLY: None of my friends ever looked very good naked.

CANON: Sally Banner, what do you really think about Australia?

SALLY: It's better to be a big frog in a small puddle.

HEADMISTRESS: Drugs, draft dodgers, demos, long hairs, abortion. What's your attitude these days, Sally Banner?

SALLY: I was a rebel in word and deed. The latter usually tones with
time.

AMPLIFIER: With time... with time... with time... with time... time...
time... time... time... time...

Music over.

Time... time...

SALLY *is spotlit downstage centre.*

SALLY: Rocking on two sticks
or down on all fours
to meet hell:
Here I am!
Bare-faced,
armoured in bone,
back at that lonely place
where I began.
Anything's possible
now that I am alone,
anything at all,
now heaven is impossible
and all's well.

The auditorium lights come up.

The SCHOOLGIRLS *march through the auditorium in twos,
singing, 'Bring Me My Bow of Burning Gold' as in the Prologue.
They pass on either side of* SALLY, *curtsey demurely to* SISTER
JUDITH, *and line up on either side of the stage.* SALLY *joins the
end of the line, straightens her back and bows to the altar.*

CANON: As it was in the beginning, is now and ever shall be.

ALL: World without end. Amen.

*A bell begins to toll and tolls at intervals throughout the rest of
the play.*

SALLY *begins to move slowly towards the chapel as the stage
darkens. A single* SCHOOLGIRL *begins to sing.*

SCHOOLGIRL: Come live with me and be my love,
And we will some new pleasures prove,
Of golden sands and crystal brooks,

With silken lines and silver hooks.
Then will the river whispering run,
Warmed by thy eyes more than the sun,
And there the enamoured fish will stay
Begging themselves they may betray.

SALLY *moves alone into the chapel. As she disappears inside, the stained-glass window lights up for the* FIRST *time. The figure of* SALLY *can be seen outlined at the top of the chapel tower.*

If thou to be seen beest loth,
By sun or moon, thou dark'nest both,
But if myself have leave to see,
I need not their light, having thee.

The bell tolls and tolls.

Towards the conclusion of the song, the SCHOOLGIRLS *file out backstage, led by the singer, and her voice dies away.*

THE END

♦ ♦ ♦ ♦ ♦ ♦ ♦ ♦

GLOSSARY

AIF: The Australian Imperial Force. The First AIF was a special volunteer force formed for overseas service in World War I. Bitter controversy over conscription followed its formation. After the war it was disbanded and reformed as the Second AIF for service in World War II.

bike, bicycle: Colloquially, a whore.

crow: A whore.

digger, dig: A form of address equivalent to 'mate', derived from the camaraderie of the Australian gold-diggings of the 1880s and 1890s; and confirmed in usage by servicemen returning from the trench warfare of World War I.

eternity: Chalked in immaculate copperplate handwriting on pavements and walls, was a familiar sight in Sydney from 1957 until the death of the pavement artist, Arthur Stace, in 1967.

four-be-two: Four-inch by two-inch timber.

OBH: A well-known seaside hotel in Perth, very fashionable in the 1940s; properly the Ocean Beach Hotel but always referred to as the OBH.

Queanbeyan: A country town in New South Wales, the town nearest to Canberra outside the Australian Capital Territory.

VJ Day: Victory over Japan; the day of the Japanese surrender in World War II, 2 September 1945.

Widgiemooltha: A small country town in Western Australia situated on the pipeline route to Kalgoorlie at the western tip of Lake Lefroy.

Young's Store: One of a chain of department stores with headquarters in Canberra.

♦ ♦ ♦ ♦ ♦ ♦ ♦ ♦

www.currency.com.au

Visit Currency Press' website now to:

- Buy your books online
- Browse through our full list of titles, from plays to screenplays, books on theatre, film and music, and more
- Choose a play for your school or amateur performance group by cast size and gender
- Obtain information about performance rights
- Find out about theatre productions and other performing arts news across Australia
- For students, read our study guides
- For teachers, access syllabus and other relevant information
- Sign up for our email newsletter

The performing arts publisher